The Greatest ☆ Skits on Earth

Other Zondervan/Youth Specialties Books

Amazing Tension Getters
Called to Care
Creative Socials and Special Events
Far-Out Ideas for Youth Groups
Good Clean Fun
Good Clean Fun, Volume 2
Great Ideas for Small Youth Groups
Greatest Skits on Earth
Greatest Skits on Earth, Volume 2
Growing Up in America
High School Ministry
High School TalkSheets
Holiday Ideas for Youth Groups
Hot Talks
Ideas for Social Action
Incredible Ideas for Youth Groups
Intensive Care: Helping Teenagers in Crisis
Junior High Ministry
Junior High TalkSheets
On Site: 40 On-Location Programs for Youth Groups
Play It! Great Games for Groups
Resource Directory for Youth Workers
Super Ideas for Youth Groups
Tension Getters
Tension Getters II
Unsung Heroes: How to Recruit and Train Volunteers
Youth Specialties Clip Art Book
Youth Specialties Clip Art Book, Volume 2

THE GREATEST

SKITS

ON EARTH

Volume Two: Skits with a Message

Wayne Rice and Mike Yaconelli

Youth Specialties

ZONDERVAN PUBLISHING HOUSE
Grand Rapids, Michigan

THE GREATEST SKITS ON EARTH
VOLUME TWO: SKITS WITH A MESSAGE
Copyright © 1987 by Youth Specialties, Inc.

Library of Congress Cataloging in Publication Data

The Greatest skits on earth.

"Youth specialties."
Contents: v. [1]. [without special title]—v. 2. Skits with a message.
Drama in Christian education. 2. Amateur plays. 3. Church work
with youth. I. Rice, Wayne. II. Yaconelli, Mike.
BV1534.4.G74   1987   246'.7   85-26608
ISBN 0-310-35211-8

All Scripture quotations, unless otherwise noted, are taken from the
Holy Bible: New International Version (North American Edition).
Copyright © 1973, 1978, 1984, by the International Bible Society.
Used by permission of Zondervan Bible Publishers.

Illustrated by Dan Pegoda
Edited by David Lambert

Printed in the United States of America

94 95 96 97 / CH / 12 11 10 9

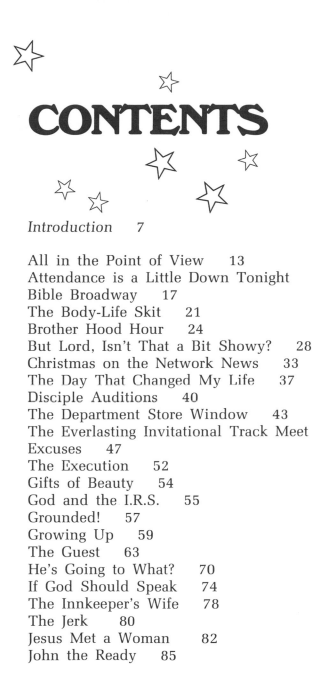

CONTENTS

Introduction   7

All in the Point of View   13
Attendance is a Little Down Tonight   15
Bible Broadway   17
The Body-Life Skit   21
Brother Hood Hour   24
But Lord, Isn't That a Bit Showy?   28
Christmas on the Network News   33
The Day That Changed My Life   37
Disciple Auditions   40
The Department Store Window   43
The Everlasting Invitational Track Meet   45
Excuses   47
The Execution   52
Gifts of Beauty   54
God and the I.R.S.   55
Grounded!   57
Growing Up   59
The Guest   63
He's Going to What?   70
If God Should Speak   74
The Innkeeper's Wife   78
The Jerk   80
Jesus Met a Woman   82
John the Ready   85

Laney Looks at the Christmas Story   89
Letters to Mama   93
LX Minutes   98
A Mad Late Date   105
Mary's Story   107
Melody in F   111
Melody in S   112
Microcosm   113
The Night Before Easter   116
Not Guilty?   118
The Offering Skit   132
Oh God!   132
Oops!   134
Palm Sunday in the News   136
Parable of the Shapes   139
The Sacrifice   146
Sayin', Doin', or Bein'   148
The $64,000 Testimony   150
Songs of the Heart   153
The Spontaneous Samaritan   159
Super-Christian to the Rescue!   160
The Tator Family   164
Today?   166
Tom Meets God   169
The Tomb Revisited   170
Whole Armor of God   174
Whose Birthday Is It?   174
The Witness   175
Witnessing, American Style   178
Would You Believe . . . ?   182

Subject Index   185

Introduction

One of the best ways to communicate with young people is to use stories—concrete examples, illustrations, pictures, anecdotes, humor.

Jesus was a master storyteller. When he wanted to communicate a difficult truth so people would understand it, he used a parable.

And who knows? He might have even used a skit or two like the ones in this book. Take, for example, the "Spontaneous Samaritan" skit on page 159. Can't you just imagine Peter and Andrew as the robbers, James and Bartholomew as the priest and the Levite, John as the Good Samaritan, and of course, Matthew as the donkey?

No? Well, maybe not.

Still, skits like the ones in this book are nothing more than parables you can see as well as hear. Not only do they help your young people learn about important issues, but they also capture and keep their attention (and the adults', too).

You'll find a great variety of skits in this book, which can be quite effective if performed appropriately. Some are short and require few props and little preparation; others are like short plays, which require sets, props, and players who will have to memorize their lines and rehearse. Most of the skits in this book are funny; some, serious.

Keep in mind that all of these skits can be adapted to fit your needs or updated. Don't hesitate to rewrite a script if it will work better for you another way.

You can use these skits in youth group meetings, morning worship or evening services at your church, or for special programs. How about a "dinner theater" on a Friday night, complete with a delicious meal served to the adults of the church by the youth, followed by a series of skits from this book? It might make a nice fund-raiser, and the church will love it!

The skits in this book differ from those in our first *Greatest Skits on Earth* book (Zondervan/Youth Specialties, 1986) because these are all intended as effective teaching tools to be followed with a discussion, Bible study, or an application of some kind. When the skit is over, ask the group to respond to questions like these: *What was the main point? Which character do you most identify with? What bothered you about this skit? What did you like?* In most cases, kids will be ready to talk after they've seen a good skit, so be prepared with discussion questions and other materials you may need.

At the end of the book is a subject index—a list of the main topics covered by the skits in this book. Use it to find appropriate skits for the subjects your youth group meetings cover. If, for instance, you already have a lesson planned on the topic of "Christian Love," then you might want to present the skit "Parable of the Shapes" on page 139 to spice up your presentation.

When choosing skit participants, try to choose people who are outgoing and who will make an effort to learn their parts well. On occasion it's a good idea to involve everyone, even those who aren't particularly good at acting, but most of the time it's best to use people who feel comfortable playing their parts and who fit the roles they are assigned. Sometimes it's best to use your adult youth sponsors as actors and actresses in these skits. Kids love to see their adult leaders "ham it up."

Some of the skits require "period" costumes and props, but for most of the skits, costumes and props can be improvised. You may want to visit a local thrift or secondhand store and stock up on some old coats, formals, hats, shoes, jewelry, and the like. Start your own "skit closet" and add to it yearly.

Many of the skits in this book appeared originally in the *Ideas* library, a set of books published by Youth Specialties. They were written or contributed by many creative people, most of them youth workers who have tried these out on their own youth groups and who understand and appreciate the value of a good skit. Our sincere gratitude to each of these contributors:

Stephen Bly
Jim Braddy
Larry Bradford
Bruce Burkholder
Bill Calvin
Bill Chaney

Ed Clements
Dick Davis
Fred Davis
David Farnum
Ted Faye
Brian Fullerton

Joe Harvey
Clyde Lee Herring
Shane Jent
Kenneth Jacobsen
Dan Johnson
Tim Johnson

Brian Kaiser
Mary Kent
Jack Klunder
Barry Kolanowski
Elaine Lidholm
David P. Mann
Luann Marter
Russ Matzke
John Meredith
Larry Michaels

Dean Nelson
Marilyn Pfeifer
Mark Reef
Carolyn Roddy
Jim Ruberg
Jean Santoiemma
Myra Shofner
Beverly Snedden
Ruth Sowpel
Lisa Swanner

Dan Van Loon
Steve Waters
Jim Wing
Len Woods
Bonnie Wright
David C. Wright
Donn Youndt
Rich Young
Tony Young

Wayne Rice and
  Mike Yaconelli

The Greatest ☆ Skits on Earth

ALL IN THE POINT OF VIEW

This skit would be excellent for a parents' night discussion-starter when both teens and their parents are present. There are actually five short vignettes that present the same situation twice—once from the parent's point of view and once from the young person's point of view. An announcer can introduce each topic before the skits are performed.

These are only samples. You can probably come up with some others of your own. If you do use these as is, encourage your actors to ad-lib as well as add their own interpretation.

	Teen Point of View	DATING		Parent Point of View
Daughter	I'm leaving now, Dad.	*Daughter*	I'm leaving now, Dad.
Father	Just where do you think you're going? What time will you be home? Who is this guy you're going with? Does he have a car? What kind? Does he have new tires on it? Did you ask your mother? What kind of job does he have? Did you brush your teeth?	*Father*	What time will you be home?
		Daughter	What's that supposed to mean? What is this, Twenty Questions? Why do you keep hounding me? Can't I get any privacy? Do you have to drill me?
Daughter	He doesn't trust me!	*Father*	It's only because I'm concerned.

	Teen Point of View	SEX	Parent Point of View
	(Daughter approaches busily working father, starts to say something, decides against it, and walks away.)		*(Father approaches busily working daughter, starts to say something, decides against it, then walks away.)*

Teen Point of View		MUSIC	Parent Point of View	
Mother	Turn down that music! *(Son turns it down.)*	*Mother*	Please turn down the music a little.	
Mother	Turn down the music! *(Son turns it down.)*	Son	WHAT!	
Mother	Turn it down!	*Mother*	Turn it down, dear.	
Son	It's off now, Mom.	Son	WHAT?	
		Mother	Never mind, dear.	
		Son	WHAT?	

Teen Point of View		PRIVILEGES	Parent Point of View	
Son	Mom, may I please borrow the car keys now?	Son	Give me the keys now.	
Mother	No way, Charlie! Not when you sit around in front of that boob tube all day and don't lift one finger to help around here.	*Mother*	I'm sorry, Son. You didn't mow the lawn like we agreed.	
Son	Yes, I know Mom, I do sometimes shirk my jobs, but I'm learning. Won't you just be understanding? I promise I'll mow the lawn tomorrow.	Son	Oh c'mon! You're not going to hold me to that, are you? *(gives a long, ridiculous excuse)*	
Mother	Stop that smart talk and get out there right this minute!	*Mother*	I'd like you to be able to use the car, but you must learn to be responsible. When you keep up your end of the bargain, I'll be happy to give you the keys.	

Teen Point of View		CHURCH	Parent Point of View	
Father	You go on to church now.	*Daughter*	Do I have to go to church today?
Daughter	Why don't you come with us, Dad?	*Father*	It would be nice to go as a family.
Father	You know this is the only day I have to sleep in.	*Daughter*	You know this is the only day I have to sleep in.
Daughter	But Dad, I think this is really important.	*Father*	Honey, I think this is really important.
Father	Well, maybe I'll watch a religious show on TV. You go on.	*Daughter*	Well, maybe I'll watch a religious show on TV. You go ahead.

ATTENDANCE IS A LITTLE DOWN TONIGHT

Here's a skit that might be appropriate if poor attendance has been plaguing your church or youth group.

Characters:	Jesus and four of his disciples: Peter, Andrew, John, and Bartholomew.
Setting:	The Upper Room

Peter: (*Peter and Andrew enter carrying articles for Passover. There is a long, narrow table on center stage.*) That should do it, Andrew. I think we have everything.

Andrew: You know, Peter, this is the first time we've not been home for Passover.

Peter: Yeh, but I'm glad we're having it with the Master. It seems to me that he hasn't been his usual self lately. Maybe this feast will cheer him up.

Andrew: He seems preoccupied with something—something that is about to happen.

Peter: I've been thinking, Andrew. Now at the time of the feast would be a great opportunity to take over the throne and set up his kingdom. The people are

	ready! You saw how they cheered for him as he rode into the city. The time of the kingdom has come and Jesus knows it!
Andrew:	Perhaps, but why is he so troubled? What is it that seems to plague his thoughts?
Peter:	To be king is no easy task, Andrew. Besides, not many of the Pharisees and priests agree with his teachings. I'm sure that bothers him.
Andrew:	But we both know that—
Peter:	*(John and Jesus enter.)* Master, everything is prepared as you requested.
Jesus:	Where are the rest of the Twelve?
Peter:	They'll be here. I gave them directions to this house. They all said they were coming except Judas. He has a business meeting somewhere. But he said he would meet us in the garden.
Andrew:	I forgot to tell you, Peter. Matthew sent a message saying that his wife wanted him to stay home with the boys tonight. And Philip told me that he's going over to Lydia's house for Passover. Master, he said to apologize to you, but he is meeting her parents tonight and—
Jesus:	*(tenderly, yet distressed)* I know, Andrew. I know.
Peter:	Say, John, where is your brother? He was supposed to help Andrew and me with the preparations.
John:	Uh, I was just telling Jesus that Father had a big catch today. James is helping mend the nets.
Jesus:	It is time for us to begin. Let's gather around the table. *(They kneel or sit.)*
Bartholomew:	*(running in)* I'm here! I'm here! You haven't started yet, have you?
Andrew:	We were just—
Bartholomew:	Good! Sorry I'm late, Jesus. But the traffic was terrible. Two donkeys hit head on in front of Ralph's Diner. It was nose to tail all the way from the temple.
John:	I thought Thomas was coming with you.
Bartholomew:	Not me!
John:	Is he coming?
Bartholomew:	I doubt it. *(pause)* Say, where is everybody?
Peter:	You tell us.
Bartholomew:	We are going to go ahead and start, aren't we? I've got to leave at 7:15.
Andrew:	Master, could we please wait for Simon the Zealot? I know he'll—

(All except Jesus grumble and say, "Oh, come on. I've got to get home" or "I've got an appointment," etc.)

John:	Hold it! I just remembered. Simon told me that a friend gave him some tickets to the arena tonight. He asked me to go, but I told him I was coming here. He said he would eat with us tomorrow.
Jesus:	Tomorrow will be too late. I have desired to eat this meal with you because I will be taken from you this night. This meal was to be a special time for us. But how can it be if you are not all here? *(distressed, not angry)*
Peter:	*(long pause)* Should we send for them, Lord?
Jesus:	No, Peter. If they loved me, they would come.

BIBLE BROADWAY

Here is a creative Broadway musical version of Acts 3. Get some costumes, learn the music and parts, and act it out for the entire church. It's fun and a great way to make this passage from the Bible come alive.

Characters:	Peter *(loud, obviously a strong leader, impatient, antsy)* John *(very easygoing and laid back, thoughtful)* Beggar #1 *(the one who gets healed—a real con artist)* Beggar #2 *(his friend)* Townspeople
The Scene:	The temple gate, called "Beautiful," at 3 in the afternoon. A few grimy beggars sit on either side of the gate looking for handouts.
Peter:	*(Enters by himself. He surveys the scene, takes a few deep breaths, and then begins to sing to the tune of "Oh What a Beautiful Morning.")* There's a bright, golden haze o'er the temple, There's a bright, golden haze o'er the temple, I feel so excited,

I can't wait to pray—
Oh, it looks like we're in for one heck of a day.

Chorus: Oh, what a marvelous feeling,
            Oh, what a beautiful gate,
            I'm in the mood for a healing. . . .

(He pauses, realizing his sidekick John is nowhere to be seen.)

Peter: *(spoken angrily)* If John doesn't come, we'll be late! John . . . JOHN! *(aside to the audience)* You'd think the guy was off in Patmos or something! (Exasperated, he huffs and goes back out the gate, out of view. From backstage, we hear: Aha! Peter reenters and announces sarcastically: Heeeeerrrrreeeeeee'sssss Johnny! John enters slowly, eating a camel burger as he trudges through the gate.)*

Peter: Egads, man! We're gonna be late for prayer. *(exasperated)* And WHY must you ALWAYS be eating? That's why you always have those weird dreams . . . you eat that spicy food this late in the day. Now c'mon!

John:	*(slowly)* Peter, Peter, Peter, or, uh, what was that the Master called you? Rocky? *(From the background, the theme from the movie Rocky blares out. The actors look surprised, then it dies out.)*
	Pete, *(putting his arm around Peter's broad shoulders in a fatherly manner)* you're always in too much of a hurry. Yup, you need to learn to take life slowly. *(spying a flower box)* You need to take time to smell . . . *(breathing deeply, then scowling and looking with disdain at the beggars)* the beggars! *(He holds his nose in mock revulsion at the beggars by the gate, on either side.)*
Beggar #2:	*(nudging #1, whispering)* He said his name's Peter.
Beggar #1:	Yeah, yeah, I heard. *(He crawls over to Peter and tugs on his robe.)*
Peter:	May I help you?
Beggar #1:	*(singing to the tune of "Hello, Dolly" background music and really hamming it up)*

Well hello, Peter,
Howdy doo, Peter
Give me money, give me silver, give me gold.
How 'bout some cash, Pete?
Hate to ask, Pete,
But my stomach is so empty,
That I'm feeling bold.

Please share the wealth, Pete!
You've got your health, Pete,
But I'm lame and I can't seem to get around.

So spell it out, Peter.
C'mon and help me out, Peter.
You know what I'm speaking of,
Give me a little o' that Christian love,
I'll be the happiest beggar in this town! *(with a flourish, winking to his buddy, obviously proud of himself)*

Peter:	*(looking sorrowfully at John, then the beggar)* Sorry, pal.
Beggar #1:	*(desperately)* Oh, pleeeeezzze!

Peter:	Read my lips. *(slowly)* No habla munero, amigo! Comprende? *(The beggar nods slowly and starts to slink away as John nudges Peter and whispers in his ear.)* BUT *(the beggar turns)* even though we're as broke as the Ten Commandments—HA HA HA *(obviously amused at his feeble attempt at humor).* Well, hit it, John!

(John produces top hats and canes, and they do a little soft-shoe to the tune of "Getting to Know You.")

> Jesus will heal you,
> He's gonna make you all better.
> You'll soon be walking,
> Thinking about where to roam.
> You won't be begging,
> Bothering us Christian leaders,
> Because of all the beautiful and new
> Things you'll be able to do
> With . . . the . . . Lord. *(They bow eagerly, cockily.)*

Peter:	*(grabs Beggar #1, raises him up while saying)* In the name of Jesus Christ the Nazarene—WALK!
Beggar #1:	*(Stands, springs, bouncing a bit, testing his ankles. He reaches down in wonderment and grabs them. Then excitedly jumps about shouting.)* I can walk! My legs . . . I'm healed, I really am! I can be somebody! *(Background music of "The Hallelujah Chorus" fills the temple. The actors all look a bit confused. Then it dies out.)*
Beggar #1:	Lights please, and give me . . . a C. *(He sings to the tune of "Sunrise, Sunset," with feeling.)*

> Are these the legs that I was born with?
> How did they get to be so strong?
> I never thought that I would walk,
> But I was wrong.

Chorus:	Walking, jumping,
Leaping, dancing,

Laughing all the day—(*Beggar #1 acts out each of these in turn, then stops suddenly, pensive.*)

Beggar #1:   Maybe I'll try out for the track team (*He jogs in place, then pauses, sobered by the thought.*)
Or maybe I'll kneel right down and pray.

(*He does so for a moment or two as the rest look reverently on, then he jumps up and the others encircle him. They all hug and chatter excitedly.*)

Peter: (*excitedly, suddenly realizing the lateness of the hour*) WHOA! The prayer time! John, c'mon before we miss THE WHOLE THING! (*They all turn and begin to try to file into the temple door over to one side of the set, but Beggar #2 blocks the way. He has felt very neglected during this whole episode and now wants to garner some of their attention and get in on all the action.*)

Beggar #2:   Wait, wait! (*He grabs the first beggar and, obviously proud of himself, begins to sing to him, a bit off-key, to the tune of "On the Street Where You Live."*)

I have often walked down this street before
Yet I've never seen you standing on your feet before
Now I want to know
How this thing is so.

(*Peter, totally frustrated at the lateness of the hour, now has pushed through the little crowd at the temple door. He physically picks up Beggar #2 and carries him out of sight into the temple as the rest quickly follow. Three or four seconds later Beggar #2 reappears in the doorway to sing his last line.*)

But I think that's the end of this show.

THE BODY-LIFE SKIT

Here's a skit for six characters based on 1 Corinthians 12. Each person who portrays a part of the body should wear a sign or T-shirt that identifies the part he is playing. The reader should have a Bible.

Characters: The reader
              The nose (shy, sneezes a lot)
              The foot (wears big shoes)
              The ear (wears earphones)
              The eye (wears big glasses)
              The head (acts conceited)

The skit begins with the body parts in a huddle.

Reader: I'll be reading selections from 1 Corinthians 12. "The body is a unit, though it is made up of many parts." *(The body parts spread apart and begin showing off their individual talents as the Reader continues.)* "And although all its parts are many, they form one body. So it is with Christ. For we were all baptized by one Spirit into one body—whether Jews or Greeks, slave or free—and we were all given the one Spirit to drink. Now the body is not made up of one part, but of many parts. If the foot should say . . ."

Foot: "Because I am not a hand, I do not belong to the body."

Reader: ". . . it would not for that reason cease to be a part of the body."

Foot: Oh yes it would. I mean, I can go places, give senior citizens rides to church, and drive for Meals on Wheels. But I can't give a lot of money like a *hand* could, or cook the best dish at the covered-dish supper like a *hand* could. Maybe I'm just not needed around here!

Reader: "And if the ear should say . . ."

Ear: "Because I am not an eye, I do not belong to the body."

Reader: ". . . it would not for that reason cease to be a part of the body."

Ear: Oh yeah? I mean, I can hear and understand a good sermon pretty well, but I can't seem to see places where anyone needs help like an *eye* could. What good is it to be able to hear and understand if you can't see to do anything? Maybe I'm just not needed around here!

Reader: "If the whole body were an eye, where would the sense of hearing be? If the whole body were an ear, where would the sense of smell be? The eye cannot say to the hand . . ."

Eye:	I don't need you, hand! I mean, *I'm* the most important part around here after all. That's pretty obvious. Anyone can see that without me, this body's just stumbling around in the dark. What good are YOU, hand?
Reader:	"Nor can the head say to the feet . . ."
Head:	Well, I don't need *any* of you. I can think and reason and make all the important decisions without any help at all from you guys. I'm the brains of this outfit.
Reader:	*(At this point, all the parts of the body begin arguing with each other so much that the Reader pleads with them to stop. The Nose moves off to the side and begins to cry.)* "On the contrary, those parts of the body that seem to be weaker are indispensable, and the parts that we think are less honorable we treat with special honor. God has combined the members of the body . . . so that there should be *no division* in the body," *(The arguing gets progressively worse.)* "but that its parts should have equal concern for each other." OH, I GIVE UP! *(Reader walks away exasperated.)*
Ear:	Hey, wait a minute. Listen! I hear someone crying. *(Everyone finally gets quiet.)*
Eye:	Look, It's _____ *(Use name of whoever is playing the nose.)* Poor guy, I wonder what's wrong.
Head:	I've got an idea! We *could* go over there and find out.
Ear:	Hey, I like the sound of that idea!
Head:	*(acting proud)* Of *course* it's a good idea.
Eye:	But how could we get there?
Foot:	I could take you, I suppose. *(There is general agreement. Everyone lines up behind the Foot, forms a train, and goes over to the Nose.)*
Ear:	*(to Nose)* We heard you crying and we're kind of worried about you. Can we help somehow?
Nose:	I don't know. I get so lonely sometimes. I wish I had some friends. But who wants to be friends with someone whose greatest talent is sniffing out trouble!
Eye:	Well, I don't know about the rest of this crew, but it seems to me that we've got some trouble that *needs* sniffing out. *(Everyone looks at the Head. Head looks sheepish.)*
Head:	Well, maybe you're right.
Foot:	You just come with us. We're not perfect yet, but when we all work *together*, we can do a lot of good after all. *(Body parts form a line with arms around each other's shoulders.)*

Reader:	*(stepping in front to read)* "If one part suffers, every part suffers with it; if one part is honored, every part rejoices with it. Now you are the body of Christ."
All:	And each one of *YOU* is a part of it!

BROTHER HOOD HOUR

Here is a humorous skit that can be used quite effectively as a discussion-starter for the topic: The Body of Christ. Set up the stage area like a typical television "talk show" and have the actors learn the lines well enough that they don't need scripts. Follow up with a discussion or study of 1 Corinthians 12:12–31.

Announcer:	And now, from Hollywood, it's *(music)* the Brother Hood Hour, featuring the inimitable Brother Johnny Hood himself! Here's Johnny!
Brother Hood:	Thank you, thank you. *(applause)* Thank you, thank you. *(applause)* THANK YOU! Have we got a show lined up for you! We have guests from around the world to discuss tonight's topic: Who or What Is the Body of Christ? So let's get started and bring on our first guest. And here he is, from Ringworm, Georgia, Mr. Foot!
Mr. Foot:	Well, hello, Brother Hood!
Brother Hood:	Mr. Foot, I can't tell you what a pleasure it is to have you on our program.
Mr. Foot:	I'm glad to be here, Brother. I bring you greetings from the N.A.E.F.
Brother Hood:	I'm sorry, but I'm not familiar with the N.A.E.F.
Mr. Foot:	A man of your caliber? I find that hard to believe! Well anyway, the N.A.E.F. is the National Association of Evangelical Feet, of which I am a charter member.
Brother Hood:	Oh, yes! As I recall, your group has recently come out with a new paraphrase of the Bible.
Mr. Foot:	Paraphrase, my foot! This is a superior translation of the Bible!
Brother Hood:	And what is it called?
Mr. Foot:	Dr. Scholl's Authorized Version. It is truly a remarkable work. This man has studied widely. He speaks eleven foreign languages, including Greek and Hebrew.

Brother Hood:	Is this in any way related to the Odor Eaters' Translation?
Mr. Foot:	No, no! The N.A.E.F. looks with disdain upon the Odor Eaters' Translation. In fact, we just think it stinks!
Brother Hood:	Well, getting down to our topic, how do you, as a Foot, feel about the rest of the body of Christ?
Mr. Foot:	Well, as a group of Feet, we feel that we have been trampled on by the rest of the body of Christ.
Brother Hood:	And what makes you feel that way?
Mr. Foot:	Let me answer that by telling you a little story. The other day at my country club—
Brother Hood:	You belong to a country club?
Mr. Foot:	Oh yes, Club Foot. Anyway, I ran into a woman that is in my Sunday school class. Do you know what she said to me? "Mr. Foot, you are a big heel!" Can you imagine that? I whipped around in holy anger and said, "Woman, you ain't got no soul!" It's just terrible the way we're treated as Feet.
Brother Hood:	I agree, that is bad! But who would you say makes up the body of Christ?
Mr. Foot:	Primarily Feet.
Brother Hood:	Would you go as far as to say that to be a member of this body you must be a Foot?
Mr. Foot:	Are you trying to buttonhole me?
Brother Hood:	Oh, no, Mr. Foot! But, surely, you must have some thoughts on the matter?
Mr. Foot:	Well, I do. I do believe you must be a Foot to be a member of the body of Christ.
Brother Hood:	Thank you, Mr. Foot. I'd like to chat with you a bit more but I must bring on our next guest. Won't you welcome with a big hand, from La Salada, Guatemala, Señor Hand! (applause)
Señor Hand:	Buenos noches, Hermano Hood.
Brother Hood:	Welcome, Señor Hand. Could you tell our audience what your occupation is?
Señor Hand:	I am professor of religion at the La Salada Universitas de los Manos.
Brother Hood:	I understand that the La Salada University of the Hands is a private school that grips the more traditional fundamentalist position. Is that true?
Señor Hand:	Sí.
Brother Hood:	How do the Hands feel about the body of Christ?

Señor Hand:	I'm so glad that you asked the question, Señor. We feel that, as Hands, we aren't getting a fair shake in the body of Christ. For some reason, we're always in hot water!
Brother Hood:	Do you feel, as a result of this, that the Hands become callous to the other members of the body?
Señor Hand:	Sí, Señor. In fact, there are some Hands that say if things don't improve, they're going to get rough!
Brother Hood:	That would be disastrous! Who do you think is the most important part in the body of Christ?
Señor Hand:	Oh, most definitely the Hands! We feel that we have a great deal of common sense—we grasp things easily.
Mr. Foot:	How can you say something like that!
Brother Hood:	Mr. Foot! Control yourself! This man is my guest and you have had your turn to speak! Señor Hand, I am so sorry!
Señor Hand:	It is all right, Hermano Hood.
Brother Hood:	Thank you for your enlightening remarks, Señor Hand. And now, may I introduce our next guest? From Canterbury-on-Avon, Worchestershire, England, Rector of the Q-tip Anglican Church, bring him on with a big hand, Reverend Ear! *(applause)* Good evening, Reverend, and welcome to the Brother Hood Hour.
Rev. Ear:	What did you say? I didn't hear you.
Brother Hood:	I said welcome to the Brother Hood Hour!
Rev. Ear:	Oh! I'm sorry! Yes, it is good to be here.
Brother Hood:	Rev. Ear, you have just written a book entitled *A History of Ears Within the Body of Christ,* published by the Earwax Press. In the book you mention, and I quote, "As a result of spiritual and social forces, Ears have become the greatest contributors to the body of Christ." Why do you say that?
Rev. Ear:	Well, I feel that Ears, as a group, have gained superiority because they are good listeners. We are indispensable to the body.
Mr. Foot:	And you call yourself a minister? That's a laugh!
Rev. Ear:	What did he say?
Brother Hood:	Please sit down, Mr. Foot! Rev. Ear, what other contributions have the Ears made?

Rev. Ear:	We have been experimenting with musical instruments and have developed a new one for worship services. It's called an ear drum.
Brother Hood:	That sounds very interesting. Do you feel that the rest of the body is deaf to these contributions?
Rev. Ear:	They are deaf only because they want to be. I believe this is because they are jealous.
Brother Hood:	Thank you, Rev. Ear, for your remarks. I'd like to discuss your book with you further, but I must bring on our next guest. Please welcome Mr. Eye from Bloodshot Hills near Lake Wawanunu, Minnesota. *(applause)* Welcome to our program, Mr. Eye.
Mr. Eye:	Thank you, Brother Hood. I'm so glad to be here. My wife thought that I didn't have the nerve to appear on national television.
Brother Hood:	I guess you'd call that optic nerve! Seriously though, Mr. Eye, we are discussing this topic: Who or What Is the Body of Christ? In general, how do the Eyes see the body of Christ?
Mr. Eye:	We believe the Eyes have it!
Brother Hood:	Why do you say that?
Mr. Eye:	Because of our great scholastic standing. We have many pupils enrolled in our schools, you know. Due to our immense contribution to academia, we feel that we are indeed the most important part of the body of Christ.
Mr. Foot:	That's it! I've had it! I'm not going to listen to any more of this garbage.
Rev. Ear:	I say, calm down old boy!
Mr. Foot:	You wanna take it outside, Parson?
Señor Hand:	You are nothing but a bully, Señor!
Mr. Foot:	Take that! *(hits him)*
Brother Hood:	Please, Mr. Foot— *(Mr. Foot hits him, too. A rumble occurs between all the guests. Brother Hood scrambles to his feet and speaks while the rumble continues.)*
Brother Hood:	Well, that's our show for tonight. We hope you enjoyed it. Tune in next week when we will be discussing the Baptism of the Holy Spirit.

BUT LORD, ISN'T THAT A BIT SHOWY?

Here's a skit about Joshua and the Battle of Jericho that contains a lot of humor as well as a message with some good discussion possibilities.

Characters:
1. The Lord
2. Joshua
3. General Beriah
4. Commander Nadab
5. Simeon
6. Ithmar
7. Caleb
8. Horn Player
9. The Curtain (Card bearer)

Hamming up the act is recommended, and costumes can be designed to fit each character. Some possibilities are yardstick swords and for helmets, football or plastic combat hats or saucepans with stars on the sides for special effect. Be creative. You'll also need to make eight cards with the following words written on them:

1. Presenting: But Lord, Isn't That a Bit Showy?
2. Next Day
3. Second Day
4. Third Day
5. Fourth Day
6. Fifth Day
7. Sixth Day
8. Seventh Day

The play begins with all characters in a huddle discussing rather loudly the battle at hand.

Joshua: All right, men, you know why we're here. We've got to take Jericho. We've been wandering around in the wilderness for forty years and now, finally, we've reached the Promised Land. But, what happens when we get here? We've got a walled city to conquer. That's why I've ordered all of you to meet with me. I thought we might come up with a plan of attack for capturing Jericho. General Beriah, what do you suggest?

Beriah: Starvation! I think we should surround the city, guard all the roads leading in, and starve them out.

Joshua: That's not a bad idea, General Beriah. It has worked before. But, there's a problem. You see, Jericho has a natural spring underneath it to provide them plenty of water. Also, our spies report that there's at least two years of grain supplies in there. I suppose we could sit around here for the next three years, but that seems to lessen our element of surprise. We need to hit fast. In three years they could have all the Canaanite armies surrounding us. Commander Nadab, what's your idea?

Nadab: I'd like to get some huge trees to use as battering rams and break down the gates. It's a worthy plan, Sir; however, there are no trees like that around here. So I don't think it will work.

Ithmar: If only Moses was here.

Joshua: *(with an irritated glance in Ithmar's direction)* Simeon, how about you? You're already ready for battle.

Simeon: I think we should just fight it out. Surround the city and start attacking. If we barrage them long enough and heavy enough with our full weapon power, we'll eventually wear them down.

Joshua: The problem with that, Simeon, is that those walls are so high and wide. We really don't have that many weapons. We need another plan.

Ithmar: I have an idea.

All: *(murmuring and nudging each other with smirks)* Ithmar has an idea!

Ithmar: I think we should build a large wooden horse and put some men inside, then when they pull the horse into the city, the men jump out and open the gates.

Joshua: Ithmar, where did you ever come up with such a thing? How about you, Caleb. What's your idea?

Caleb: Besiege the wall around the city. Then we could go right over the top. Here's how we could do it. Find every basket we can and fill it with dirt. Get our men to carry them right up to the wall and dump them as fast as we can. We'd have a ramp in no time.

Joshua: That's great!

Lord:	Joshua. *(The Lord is offstage; only his voice is heard.)*
Joshua:	*(looking around curiously)* Huh? What?
Lord:	*(louder)* Joshua!
Joshua:	*(moving off by himself)* Uh, just a minute, men. Take ten.
Ithmar:	*(annoyed)* I sure wish Moses was here.
Joshua:	Yes, Sir?
Lord:	What do you think you're doing?
Joshua:	We're planning our attack against Jericho, Sir.
Lord:	What have you decided?
Joshua:	Our ideas? Well, we were going to starve them, then we thought we'd attack them head on. Now we're discussing a possible siege work.
Lord:	Did Ithmar contribute an idea?
Joshua:	Ithmar? Well, uh, yes Sir. He had this thing about a wooden horse.
Lord:	I wonder where he learned to read Greek. As your commander-in-chief, may I make a suggestion?
Joshua:	You have an idea for us? Thank you, Lord. Wait a minute, I'll get something to write on. Hey, men, he's got an idea for us! *(pointing up)* All right, I'm ready.
Lord:	First day. Get all the mightiest men together.
Joshua:	Right!
Lord:	March around the city.
Joshua:	Got it.
Lord:	Take the rest of the day off.
Joshua:	You gotta be kidding!
Lord:	I'm not much of a kidder, Joshua. Second day, same thing! Third day, same thing. Do that for six days. Then, the seventh day march around the city seven times, shout, and the city's yours!
Joshua:	No offense, Lord, but this plan is the pits. We just shout and the whole thing collapses? Lord, I don't know. The men aren't going to believe this. Don't you think that's a bit overdramatic?
Lord:	*(clearing throat first)* Joshua, did you have anything to do with the plagues in Egypt?
Joshua:	No, Sir, I didn't.
Lord:	Did you have anything to do with the parting of the Red Sea?
Joshua:	No, Sir, you did it.

Lord:	Did you have anything to do with the manna in the wilderness?
Joshua:	No, Sir.
Lord:	Do you know how to strike a rock and make water gush forth?
Joshua:	No, Sir. And I didn't have anything to do with the burning bush or parting the waters of the Jordan.
Lord:	I have a reputation for doing things a bit differently, you might say, and I'm batting 1000 by the way.
Joshua:	*(rolling eyes)* All right, I get the drift. We'll do it your way. *(rejoining men)* O.K., men, I've got another plan here.
Ithmar:	I know! We're going to build a giant hollow camel!
Joshua:	NO! O.K.? And I wish you'd quit saying, "If only Moses was here." Moses isn't here, but I am and I'm in charge. Moses disappeared up on that mountain, and we haven't seen him since. I'm sure he's dead. Anyway, men, here are the orders. In the morning get your best soldiers and equip them in full armor—swords, spears, shields, everything. Have them lined up by dawn. Ithmar, you get the horn act together with your first horn player. We'll be carrying the ark of the covenant. We'll march around the city single file, and everyone is to be absolutely quiet. Then, you get the rest of the day off. *(All show signs of disbelief and amazement, some murmuring.)*
Joshua:	That's right. The second day we'll do the same thing. Got it? We'll do this six days in a row, then on the seventh day we'll march around the city seven times. While everyone faces the city and the horn plays extra loud, we'll shout and the, uh, walls will, uh, tumble down. Now I know it sounds wild, but we're going to do it just like he said. If it doesn't work, it's his fault, not ours. See you in the morning. *(All sack out around the stage. The curtain moves across stage with #2 card. Horn sounds out reveille. Everyone except Ithmar starts getting up.)*
Joshua:	O.K., everybody up. Let's go. Get in line there. We've got to look in top shape. One time around the city, men. And everyone quiet, except for the blowing of that horn. That is a horn, isn't it? Where's Ithmar? *(Ithmar wanders up.)* Ithmar, you slept in.
Ithmar:	You know what, Joshua? I think Moses is alive and well and living on the Riviera.
Joshua:	ITHMAR! Do you have the horn number ready to go?
Ithmar:	*(shrugs shoulders and gets in line)* Yes.

Joshua: (*all marching around a portion of the room*) O.K., let's go. Once around the city. Hup, two, three, four. Keep smiling! All the way around, Ithmar. Blow the horn! O.K., that's it, men. Same time, same place tomorrow. (*The curtain holds up #3 card.*)

Joshua: All right, men. Everyone in line. Now, remember, just once around the city.

Beriah: Did you see the way they looked at us yesterday? They hung all over the walls wondering what we were up to.

Joshua: (*talking to himself*) Sometimes I wonder! (*to men*) Now, here we go . . . hup, two, three, four. (*Characters continue to march while the curtain moves across stage showing cards #4 through #8.*)

Joshua: (*Men stop briefly.*) Whew! Well, men, this is it. This is our big day. I hope you're in shape. Seven times around the city, but keep it quiet. Horn, your big number is on the seventh lap. Then everyone turns, shouts, and watches. All right, men, keep in step. Hup, two, three, four. Hup, hup, hup, hup. That's once. Keep it up. Hup, hup. Play that horn! That's twice . . . and three times. Four times. Five . . . six . . . seven times. All right, let her rip! Everyone shout! (*All shout.*) It worked! Uh, *CHARGE*, men. Take the city! Ithmar, did you see that?

Lord: Joshua!

Joshua: (looking up) Huh? Oh! Go on, Ithmar. (waves him offstage) Yes, Sir! Did you see that? It's amazing. What a great plan!

Lord: Joshua, cool your heels and get this down.

Joshua: Oh, yes Sir. I'll write it down.

Lord: Total, strict obedience to the Lord produces amazing, dramatic effects.

Joshua: That's great. Thank you, Lord. I won't forget that, no Sir!

Lord: Well, they don't call me omnipotent for nothing. And, uh, Joshua, tell Ithmar that Moses is up here with me.

Joshua: (with wide grin and then a glance toward exit) Ithmar! Hey Ithmar, I've got news.

CHRISTMAS ON THE NETWORK NEWS

Presented as a newscast on the evening news, this skit could be videotaped to simulate an actual television program. Your group might want to build a TV news set, with desks, station call letters in the back, and so forth. The "news," of course, is the Christmas story; the newscast occurs on the first Christmas day in a modern setting, so all the news commentators should be dressed in today's clothes. Feel free to adapt this skit to meet the needs of your group.

Announcer: Stay tuned for the VBS Evening News with Barnabas Cronkite reporting the latest on a strange sighting in the sky, Martha Waltersberg from downtown Bethlehem, where a huge crowd is gathering for a tax enrollment, and Dr. Ben Hadad with reports about a new cold front moving in. That's the VBS News coming up next.

Commercial: Taxes. Taxes. Taxes. No one likes to pay taxes. Especially when H & R Blockberg can help you pay the least taxes possible. H & R Blockberg is the only tax-consulting service authorized by the Roman government; each and every consultant has previous tax collecting experience. Yes, you can trust H & R Blockberg for all your tax-related problems. H & R Blockberg, 700 Appian Way.

Announcer: The VBS Evening News with Barnabas Cronkite in Jerusalem, Martha Waltersberg in Bethlehem, and Dr. Ben Hadad on Mt. Ararat. Brought to you by Hertz Donkey Rental—the Donkeys O.J. Feldman rides—and Gethsemane Nurseries, with gardens in every major city. Now . . . Barnabas Cronkite.

Barnabas:	Good evening. There has been a new development on the strange light that has been sighted in the eastern hemisphere for the last few nights. Correspondent Moshe Smith reports.
Moshe:	For the past few nights a bright light or starlike phenomena has been appearing in the sky. At first it was thought to be a meteor or an optical illusion, but tonight Dr. Ishmael Streisand confirmed that what everyone is seeing is, in fact, a star. The question is, Where did this star come from and what does it mean? Officials close to the situation are speculating that the star is not an isolated incident and that more strange occurrences may be expected. Concerned government officials are monitoring the situation closely, and reliable sources have told VBS that other incidents have not been made public. This is Correspondent Moshe Smith in Jerusalem.
Barnabas:	VBS News has learned that an incident did occur near Bethlehem, and we now switch to our minicam. Live in the hills of Bethlehem, David Saul reports.
David:	Barnabas, approximately ten minutes ago a group of shepherds told me that they saw some kind of an angel accompanied by music and bright lights. Normally, stories from shepherds are discounted because of the fact that they are a strange breed and tend to hit the sauce, *but* government officials here seem strangely concerned. From my discussions with the shepherds, apparently, they think this has something to do with a messiah promised years ago. The mention of a messiah seems to be what has government officials so concerned. From the hills of Bethlehem, this has been David Saul reporting.
Barnabas:	We'll be right back after this message from Hertz.
Commercial:	O.J. Feldman here for Hertz. When you're in a strange town, it's nice to know your friends at Hertz are ready to help. Maybe you had to trade in your donkey because you needed tax money or because he kicked people in crowds, that's the time to rent a donkey from Hertz. Our donkeys like crowds and are guaranteed to get you where you want to go. Of course, Hertz uses nothing but fine GMAC donkeys. Hertz—where we treat donkeys like donkeys and treat people right.
Barnabas:	Last month Caesar Augustus issued a decree requiring all citizens to return to their cities of birth to attain an accurate enrollment for taxing. Martha Waltersberg is in Bethlehem for the story.

Martha:	I'm standing here at the No Room Inn on the outskirts of Bethlehem. Thousands of people are swarming into the city now and every available facility is full. Just a few minutes ago a woman who is about to have a baby was almost turned away. Finally, after protests from her husband, they were allowed to stay with the animals. We just finished talking with the head of the Best Eastern Lodge Association, and he suggests that anyone heading for Bethlehem attempt to find lodging outside of town. The head of the Roman government here in Bethlehem is deeply concerned about crowd control. So far, there have not been any major incidents. The question is, Can this uneasy quiet continue? Martha Waltersberg at the No Room Inn in Bethlehem.
Barnabas:	A group of highly respected astrologers have begun a significant journey. Correspondent Mort Solomon reports from Peking.
Mort:	Barnabas, a large party of wealthy astrologers is traveling toward Israel to observe a strange light. Apparently, it is the same strange light seen over Israel the past few weeks. Informed sources have told us that these men believe there is some relation between the light and the Messiah. Although there has been no official recognition by the Roman government, it is believed that when the astrologers arrive within Roman territory, they will be summoned before government officials. Reporters here, Barnabas, are baffled as to this sudden concern on the part of Roman officials for the promised Messiah. Why, we just will have to wait and see. Mort Solomon from China.
Commercial:	The VBS News will continue in just a moment. Ladies, now is the time to order your hooded capes and robes. The Good Hood Company has an incredible selection of hooded capes and robes that are all one piece of material. No longer can your hood be lost or entangled in water jugs being carried on the head. The Good Hood Company, where we also have a clearance on beautiful sheepskin swimming suits. Come by and see us soon.
Barnabas:	Eric Rosen has been watching with interest the increasing speculation about a coming messiah. Eric.
Eric:	The reason there is so much concern about a messiah, of course, is the popular notion by the Jews that such a messiah will become a political force and overthrow the Romans. This is a hope that Jews have had for years, and we have seen potential "messiahs" come and go. We have a feeling that the strange light

in the East is nothing more than a passing phenomena that those who are overly religious and mystical can cling to or, worse yet, use to mount a revolutionary movement. I have done some research on the matter of a messiah and I am not so sure that if and when such a savior were to appear, he would be a political leader. I am sure I will get a lot of mail about this, but I think it would be much more profitable if those who are so anxiously awaiting the Messiah would start living like they believed in the God they say they do. I guess it is always easier and less threatening to hope in the future than to live like the future were now. Eric Rosen, VBS News.

Barnabas: Jerusalem has been the home of the National Open Spear Throwing Olympics. Stud Barjonas reports.

Stud: Coming from major upset victories, two Hebrews will be facing each other in the finals to be held next Friday. Friday's match between Philip of Caesarea and Simeon of Bethany has already been sold out. There is some concern that Philip of Caesarea may have trouble keeping his feet within the specified boundaries on his approach. He refused comment on the two warnings he received today. However, sources close to Philip confirm that he will be wearing a new imported brand of sandal to give him additional footing. Should be quite a match. In chariot racing today, Fireball Jonah narrowly escaped serious injury when his vehicle turned over in the north-west turn at the Hippodrome. This turn is considered one of the most hazardous in racing. In spite of the mishap, Jonah went on to win the main event.

Barnabas: Dr. Ben Hadad has been standing by on Mt. Ararat for the weather report, but we have just received a bulletin from Bethlehem. Martha Waltersberg is there.

Martha: Barnabas, as you know from my earlier report, I am at the No Room Inn here in Bethlehem. Just as we were getting ready to leave, we were told of a commotion at the back of the inn. We found a young girl who had just given birth to a baby where they keep the animals. Normally, we would have ignored the story, but, Barnabas, something strange is occurring here. A huge crowd is gathering and a number of shepherds and others almost seem to be worshiping the baby. We have been unable to get any comment from anyone here, but there is one other thing. That strange light in the East seems to be much brighter now and almost seems to be directly above us. This is Martha Waltersberg in a stable in Bethlehem.

Barnabas: And that's the way it is. Barnabas Cronkite for the VBS Evening News. Good night.

THE DAY THAT CHANGED MY LIFE

The following script is a dramatic presentation based on the life of Zacchaeus, the tax collector. In scene 1 costumes from biblical times would be appropriate for Zacchaeus and the other characters. Scene 2 is essentially a monologue for Zacchaeus.

This presentation would be an excellent way to present the gospel message.

Scene 1: *Zacchaeus sits or stands behind a table. A man with his wife stops by to pay their taxes, but they don't have enough money. Zacchaeus presses them to pay the entire amount or go to jail. They reluctantly pay with money they were going to use for food. The couple walks off.*

Zacchaeus: Thank you, and have a good day! *(singing "I'm in the money. I'm in the money.")*

Scene 2: Zacchaeus is alone on stage.

Zacchaeus: My name is Zacchaeus and that's what I used to be like before I met a man named Jesus. I am the chief tax collector at Jericho. That means I have several tax collectors working for me.

I am a very important person and I used to be very corrupt. We would overcharge people for their taxes, and all of us would get a share of the excess. Of course, I would get the biggest share!

I became a very wealthy man. But I became colder and harsher with every ill-gotten gain. My heart was hardened and I didn't care about people anymore. My life was money and I always wanted more. And I always got what I wanted. But that was before I met Jesus. Let me take you back to the day that changed my life.

One day everyone in Jericho was very excited and talking about this man named Jesus who was approaching our city. I had heard a lot about him—what a wise teacher he was and about some miracles he had done—curing many who had diseases, sicknesses, and evil spirits, giving sight to many who were blind, and bringing the dead back to life. Some said he even had the power to forgive people's sins.

I had to see this for myself. So I locked up the money that we had collected and began to follow the crowd.

There were so many people there that I couldn't get close to the city gate. But I heard that he had already entered Jericho and would be passing by soon. I also heard that Jesus had just restored the sight of a blind beggar just outside our city and that he was with Jesus, too.

Then someone shouted, "There he is!" and I began to push my way through the crowd. Well, as you can see, I am not a very big man and as the crowd pushed back, I found myself right where I had started—still unable to see.

The noise of the people became louder, and I knew Jesus was just passing by. I ran over to a nearby sycamore tree and climbed it as fast as I could. I felt a little foolish—with my fancy robe and all—but for some reason I had to see this man from Galilee.

I got up into the tree just in time to see him coming. He was walking along talking with the people. A great crowd was following him by now. My heart started pounding as he approached, and as he drew closer, he looked up and saw me.

As all the people followed his eyes upward, Jesus called out my name, "Zacchaeus!" How did he know my name? We had never met. I was so caught off guard that I missed what he said next, and he had to repeat it. "Zacchaeus, come down here, for today I'm going to stay at your house."

For some reason I felt something within me change. Jesus was a man known for his compassion. And I was overcome by that love—just by looking at him and hearing him call my name.

But Jesus was also recognized for his authority. He seemed to be in charge. But not by taking advantage of people—like I had done—but by loving them. And this was the first time I had ever felt this kind of love.

I hurried down the tree and welcomed him gladly. He embraced me, we sat down, and he started asking me some questions. As we talked, some people started grumbling, "He has gone to be the guest of a sinner." They were probably *so* looking forward to Jesus staying at *their* homes. And, of course, they *weren't* sinners!

When I heard this talk, I stood up and said to Jesus—loud enough so that everyone could hear me—"Look, Lord! Here and now I give half of my possessions to the poor, and if I have cheated anybody out of anything, I will pay back *(pause)* four times the amount."

A hush came over the crowd and I heard some people gasp. They started whispering to each other. Probably doubting my sincerity, or figuring out how much I was to pay them!

Then Jesus stood up and said, "Today salvation has come to *this* house, because this man, too, is a son of Abraham. For the Son of Man came to seek and to save what was lost."

That was a great day for me. Yes, Jesus did stay at my house that evening. And when he left the next day, he *continued* to stay in this house *(pointing to his heart)*. His spirit has been with me ever since. And I count it a privilege to be called one of his followers. I also consider myself to be very fortunate.

You see, when Jesus left Jericho, he went to Jerusalem. I never saw Jesus again because it was then and there that he was crucified. It's hard to say if any other man's voice would have changed my life the way Jesus' did when he called my name. One thing *is* for certain: I knew what I had to do when I was face to face with him and he said, "Zacchaeus." And I did it.

I learned three things that day:

For one, I learned that I could overcome any physical limitation if my desire to reach my goal was great enough. How great is *your* desire to see Jesus? What is standing in your way of seeing him? I also learned that my past sins can be made right and that I can be forgiven. And I learned that when Jesus calls your name, it's never too late to answer yes, but that *now* is the best time.

Jesus is calling your name today/tonight. Will you answer yes to him?

DISCIPLE AUDITIONS

For this skit, you will need eight auditioners, one stagehand, and the director. This dialogue is only meant to give you an outline to follow. Have your actors ad-lib their own lines to fit their parts.

Director:	Thank you for coming, ladies and gentlemen. As you know, we are auditioning for disciples to follow Jesus Christ. When your number is called, please step forward to the microphone and answer the questions.
Stagehand:	Number One, please. *(Person #1 steps to the microphone. She should obviously be a "glamour girl" type.)*
Director:	State your name, please.
Person #1:	*(Use real or ficticious names.)*
Director:	Why do you want to be a disciple?
Person #1:	Well, isn't this a beauty contest? I thought you would obviously want me. I'm so gorgeous!
Director:	Thank you, Miss. Step back, please.
Stagehand:	Number Two, please.
Director:	State your name. *(He does.)* Louder, please. *(Again, he does.)* Thank you, Mr. _____, why do you want to be a disciple?
Person #2:	Well, actually, I don't know. My mother made me come and if I didn't show up, I'd get so much flack it wouldn't be worth it. I'm here because I have to be here.
Director:	Thank you. You may step back.
Stagehand:	Number Three, please.
Director:	State your name, please. *(He does.)* And why do you want to be a disciple?

Person #3:	Well, I'm really good at everything. I'm an honor student, a member of the basketball team, and first chair in band. You name it and I can do it. So, here I am.
Director:	Thank you. Step back, please.
Stagehand:	Number Four.
Director:	Your name, please? *(He gives his name.)* What? *(Again, he gives his name.)* O.K., Mr. _____, why do you want to be a disciple?
Person #4:	I need a job. I'm in trouble. I broke my bike. I need new shoes. Please, take me. I'll work hard. Honest!
Director:	Thank you. Please step back.
Stagehand:	Next—Number Five.
Director:	Number Five, state your name. *(She does.)* Why do you want to be a disciple?
Person #5:	Well, I'm not very good at anything, but if Jesus can use me, I'll do whatever he wants.
Director:	Thank you, Miss _____. Step back.
Stagehand:	Number Six.
Director:	State your name. *(He does.)* Why do you want to be a disciple?
Person #6:	Well, I've been in Sunday school for fourteen years. I go to Bible study on Tuesday, youth group on Wednesday, and I help with the children's program on Saturday. I attend all three services on Sunday, and I never miss anything. I know what discipleship means.
Director:	And what does it mean?
Person #6:	To be a follower—I follow all my friends and know when everything meets.
Director:	Thank you, step back.
Stagehand:	Number Seven, please.
Director:	State your name, please. *(She does.)* And why do you want to be a disciple?
Person #7:	I don't have an option. I've decided to follow Christ, and he has commanded me to go and to make disciples. And to make disciples, I guess I have to be one.
Director:	Thank you, Miss _____. Step back, please.
Stagehand:	Number Eight, step forward.
Director:	State your name, please. *(very shy response)* Don't be afraid. Say your name loud and clear. *(He does.)* O.K., why do you want to be a disciple?

| Person #8: | I don't understand what it means, but I want to know Jesus better and I was hoping you would help me. |
| Director: | Thank you. Step back, please. I'd like to ask all of you to leave the room for a moment, while I discuss the decision with my associate. *(They all leave.)* |

At this point, the director mumbles something to the stagehand, and the stagehand leaves to bring back Numbers One, Two, Three, Four, and Six.

Director:	I have reached my decision. When I call your number, please step forward.
	Number One, Miss _____. So you think this is a beauty contest. Being a disciple has nothing at all to do with what you look like on the outside. It's who you have in the inside that counts. Thank you for auditioning. I'm sorry.
	Number Two. Your mother made you come, Mr. _____ ? Well, this is one thing your mother can't make you do. You can only do it on your own. Thank you for auditioning. You may leave.
	Number Three, Mr. _____. It's great that you can do everything. Unfortunately, being a disciple has little to do with what you can do, but rather what you can't do. That's why a disciple needs Jesus. Thank you for auditioning.
	Number Four. So you want a job. You need the money. Well, discipleship will cost you everything you have for maybe no money gained at all. But the final reward is great. Thank you for auditioning.
	Number Six. Ah yes, you follow your friends to every meeting. But the question is, Do you follow Jesus? What do you do for him?
Person #6:	What do you mean? As long as I go to everything, isn't that enough?
Director:	A disciple joyfully does whatever he can for Jesus with or without his friends. Thank you for auditioning.
Director:	Stagehand. *(leaves and brings in Numbers Five, Seven, and Eight)*
Director:	Number Five, step forward. Miss _____. You love Jesus but can't do anything? You have a special talent that God has given you for discipleship. Welcome to the family.

Number Eight, step forward. You want to learn more about Jesus. We're here to help a learner learn more. You see, that's what discipleship is all about. Welcome to the family.

Number Seven. Ah yes, the girl with no option. You're right. You accepted Christ and to follow his command, you are a disciple. Thank you for coming and welcome to the family.

(to stagehand) Why are so many called and so few chosen?

Stagehand: Don't worry. Look at all these people *(pointing to audience)*. Perhaps next time, some of these folks will audition. I think we'll get a better result.

THE DEPARTMENT STORE WINDOW

This is a Christmas pantomime. No words are spoken.

The scene: A store window
Characters: 1 Window dresser
2 Window washers
Several mannequins—an angel, 1 or 2 shepherds, Mary, Joseph, 1 or 2 Wisemen, 2 sheep (Use the pastor or youth pastor here—the kids will love it.)
Props: Manger, hay, doll in manger (baby), other nativity scene props, such as shepherds' staffs, gifts for the Wisemen, etc., and window-washing equipment

The scene opens with the mannequins at the back of the stage with their backs to the audience, in bare feet and dressed in the appropriate robes (wearing shorts, no pant legs showing). The two window washers are stage front and have sponges, squeegees, buckets, overalls, caps, etc. They are washing a huge window that covers the whole front of the stage. These two characters should be chosen for their ability to be real hams (spitting on the window when they can't get a spot off, etc.). After a few minutes, one goes off stage and washes the window from the inside, matching the other's motions. The actors should have a lot of fun with this part and draw laughter from the audience.

After a little while, a woman window dresser enters from backstage with a pencil behind her ear and a clipboard under her arm, dressed obviously like a businesswoman. Ignoring the window washers at first, she drags a large box to stage right that is full of scarves, crowns, halos, and other nativity props. Just off stage, out of sight but easily accessible, should be two chairs, the manger, a doll, staffs, etc. (the larger props). The dresser then steps backward (toward the audience), takes a look at what she has to work with, and then goes to the mannequins and drags some backward to stage front. *All mannequins must lock their knees, feigning dead weight and staying absolutely still.* One of the shepherds can be brought out first and positioned to the right of the stage near the front. As she tries to adjust him into position—hands, head, legs, etc., she realizes she could use the help of the window washers. She mimes talking to the one on the inside. He agrees and she motions the other one to come inside. Both washers join her and drop all their equipment backstage before continuing.

Mannequins start here, file in backward.

1 Shepherd #1
2 Wiseman
3 Shepherd #2
4 Mary
5 Joseph
6 Sheep #1
7 Sheep #2
8 Angel
9 Manger

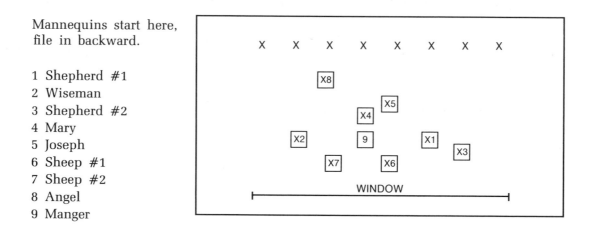

As the dresser has the washers drag mannequins one by one to places she indicates (see diagram), she meanwhile adds a sash here, a headpiece there, a scarf here and there—never dressing one mannequin completely—so that the audience is not aware of the nativity scene yet. The whole procedure of positioning the mannequins takes quite a while, and the key to its success is the ability of the window washers to ham it up while the dresser seeks to seriously arrange her display. Every time her back is turned or she is involved with a mannequin, the washers goof around by sticking fingers of mannequins in their noses, raising their arms and holding their noses, etc. The more laughs the better. The washers would be doing this between dragging around the mannequins as directed by the dresser. As the dresser keeps discovering their antics, she keeps shooing them to the side, shaking her head and putting the mannequins back in position. The dresser should also change her mind a few times and have the washers move mannequins back or forward a few inches as if she is really arranging a display.

When Mary is brought out, the dresser should have a chair brought out for her to sit on. The last mannequin to be brought out should be the angel. The angel should be one of the last to be completely dressed in a white robe and with a halo on her head. Then she should be lifted up (knees locked) on another chair by the two washers.

A word of caution: As this pantomime can take quite a while, be careful not to have the angel spread her arms out to the side too soon or she will not be able to hold that position. The same goes for the other mannequins. Keep everyone in easy positions until just before the end when some last-second adjusting can be done.

Only after all the characters are positioned, place the final headpieces on the mannequins, then get the gifts, staffs, and have the washers bring out the manger and doll. The dresser motions her thanks and shoos the washers, taking the box with them, off stage. The dresser does any final arranging needed and when clearly satisfied, leaves the stage.

The house lights go off. The spotlights come on, and a soloist then sings two verses of "O Holy Night" or "Silent Night." The impact is dramatic.

See diagram to show how the stage can be set up.

THE EVERLASTING INVITATIONAL TRACK MEET

Here's a skit based on Hebrews 12:1—4 that involves five people (the Reporter and four track team members).

Setting: Locker-room interview before a track meet

Reporter: *(dressed like a TV news reporter with a microphone)* Good evening, ladies and gentlemen, this is sportscaster Sammy Secularist welcoming you to the Everlasting Invitational Track Meet. Before the competition begins today, I would like to take you inside the locker room of the "Maranatha Marathoners," a very strange but interesting group of athletes. They claim to be citizens of "another kingdom"—whatever that means—and for the most part have a victorious team year after year. Let's go now and see if we can get some insight into their success. *(knocks on door)*

#1:	Come in. *(Team is doing stretching exercises.)*
Reporter:	Hi! I was just wondering if you would be willing to answer a few questions concerning your motivation and strategy for the race today.
Everyone:	Sure, we'd be glad to.
Reporter:	As all racing fans know, this event has two courses to choose from. Why do you always take the narrow path instead of the more popular broad, scenic route?
#1:	Well, we're often criticized for that. Most of the other runners take the scenic route. They say it's more exciting and, granted, it is more of a crowd pleaser. But we have our course marked out for us, so we just press on toward the goal to win our prize!

Reporter:	You mean that beautiful gold trophy?
#1:	No, I'm talking about a crown that will last forever.
Reporter:	Oh, yeah. *(not understanding and turning to the next person)* Since you've chosen the difficult track, there must be times when you get tired and feel like quitting. How do you deal with that temptation?
#2:	I just think of that great cloud of witnesses who have completed this same race before me.
#3:	Yeah, and most of them suffered more than we ever will. When I see what they endured, it encourages me to keep running!
Reporter:	You all seem very dedicated. I guess you have to be pretty good to make this team, right?
#4:	Not really. We were all in pretty bad shape when our coach chose us.
Reporter:	I don't understand.
#4:	Well, our coach is known for inviting the least likely candidates to join the team.
#3:	And once you join, he's like a father. He spends time with you and teaches you the rules and strategies from his handbook. And before you know it, you're off and running!
Reporter:	So he's more than a coach. In fact he sounds like more than just a man. What's his name?
#2:	His name is Jesus, the author and perfector of our faith. We keep our eyes fixed on him. IIe is the reason we run. Hey! Why don't you run with us? It won't be in vain! And we promise you, you'll win!
Reporter:	I'm in terrible shape, but . . . I guess you-know-who will take care of that, right? *(pause)* From the Everlasting Invitational Track Meet, this is Sammy Secularist, uh, make that just Sammy, saying so long for now!

EXCUSES

If you have had trouble recruiting leadership in your church, here is a creative and fun way to get people thinking. *Excuses* is a singing-commercial skit that can be presented by your youth to the adults.

Characters: Chairman of nominating committee
Nervous Nell
Hypochondriac Herman
Society Sue
Tired Timothy
Sunday school Superintendent
Tardy Tilly
Hostess Hortense
Last-Minute Melvin

Props: *(All wear signs stating their names.)* Nervous Nell—large handkerchief; Hypochondriac Herman—hot water bottle and large bottle of pills; Society Sue—gaudy hat, jewelry, fur and lorgnette; Tired Timothy—make-up of tired lines; Tardy Tilly—hair curlers, furry slippers, coat; Hostess Hortense—apron, cooking spoon; Last-Minute Melvin—bathrobe; poster, telephone, cardboard letters

SCENE 1:

(All sing in unison to tune of "A-Tisket A-Tasket.")

> Excuses, excuses, we always get excuses,
> When we ask some folks to help,
> We always get excuses!

(Each member sings one line and holds up a corresponding cardboard letter. Song is sung to tune of "Rock-A-Bye, Baby.")

> E-mbarrassed to try it,
> X-cuse me this year,
> C-hildren upset me,
> U-lcers, my dear,
> S-imply too nervous,
> E-xhausted you see,
> S-ad nominating committee!

Chairman: *(sings to tune of "Ten Little Indians")*

One little, two little, three little excuses
Everyone is blowing their fuses,
Putting their talents to other uses,
On a Sunday morning.

Nervous Nell: *(enters shaking, biting nails, and wringing hankie and sings to tune of "She'll Be Coming 'Round the Mountain")*

I just can't teach a class when I come,
I get so nervous, and my legs get numb,
If I were prepared,
Then I wouldn't be so scared,
But those children always make me feel so dumb!

Hypochondriac Herman: *(enters carrying hot water bottle in one hand and large bottle of pills, or thermometer, in the other hand and sings to tune of "Old Black Joe")*

Gone are the days when my heart was young and gay,
My health's so bad, may not live out the day,
Don't count on me, I hate to make you sad,
I know you need a teacher, but I feel too BAD!

Society Sue: *(enters peering condescendingly through lorgnette at audience and sings in high falsetto with rolled r's to tune of "Jingle Bells")*

Every day, PTA,
Brownies or the troop,
I am just so busy now,
My calendar is pooped.
Can't take a class, so I'll pass,
Ask another time.
Maybe I can work it in,
In 1999!

Tired Tim:	(*enters with slumped shoulders, slow gait, and sighs loudly before singing to tune of "I've Been Workin' on the Railroad"*)

I have been a superintendent
For the past ten years,
Through the joys and through the sorrows,
The laughter and the tears.
Now my bones are getting weary,
I just can't work so hard.
Get a younger man to do it,
'Cause I am just too 'tard!

SCENE 2:

Scene opens with a pianist playing "Reveille" and with someone displaying a poster that says, "Later on Sunday mornings we hear . . ."

Superintendent:	(*paces back and forth, looks at his watch, and sings to tune of "Where Has My Little Dog Gone?"*)

Oh where, oh where, can the teacher be,
Oh why, oh why aren't they here?
It's a quarter to ten and they haven't come in,
Oh why did they not appear?

Tardy Tilly:	(*runs in breathless with coat only on one arm and sings to tune of "Old McDonald Had a Farm"*)

I forgot my teacher's book,
E-I-E-I-O
I left it on the breakfast nook,
E-I-E-I-O
With a rush-rush here,
And a rush-rush there,
Brush my teeth and comb my hair,
And couldn't find a thing to wear,
E-I-E-I-O!

Superintendent:	(still paces and looks at his watch, glances at the phone, and sings to tune of "Are You Sleeping?")

Are they swimming, hedges trimming?
Did they call, did they call?
Picnicking or snoring, they are still ignoring
Their duty, their duty.

Hostess Hortense:	(enters and dials phone, sings to tune of "Reuben, Reuben")

I won't be at church this morning.
I would like to, but I can't,
In just walked my father, mother,
Brother, sister, uncle, and aunt.
I would like to bring them with me,
But their visits are so rare,
I must give them all my free time,
So I guess I won't be there.

Last-Minute Melvin:	(enters in bathrobe, hair disheveled, dials phone, sings to tune of "Farmer in the Dell")

Herman lost his shoe.
Matilda drank the glue.
Little Fred is in bed.
We think he's got the flu!

(all singing to the tune of "Oh Susanna")

Now everyone has sung his song,
And we must bid adieu,
But we are hoping that we brought
A little laugh or two.
You've seen excuses
In jest, but still they're true.
Now aren't you glad that you are here,
So we can't sing about you!

THE EXECUTION

This skit is a good discussion-starter about the meaning of the crucifixion of Christ. It requires two actors who have speaking parts and any number of others who carry out the actions described in the column marked "Visual" below. These actions take place behind the actors while they are talking, and the actors seem totally oblivious to what is going on behind them.

VISUAL	AUDIO
Camera (or spotlight) on men eating lunch.	*Calvinicus:* Hi, George. What's new?
	Georgius: What d'ya mean? Nothing ever happens around here. Looks like another hot one. Nice day for camels, eh?
	Calvinicus: (*chuckles*) Yeah, pass me an olive, will ya?
	Georgius: Here you are, ya beggar. Why don't you get yourself a bowl and sit at the Jerusalem gate?
	Calvinicus: Lay off, O.K.? It's been rough enough today out there in the fields. Look at these fingernails!
People start walking across behind the workmen.	*Georgius:* Yeah, I know. The ground is so hard. Almost broke the yoke right off my ox.
	Calvinicus: What's going on anyway? What's all this commotion about?
	Georgius: Oh, just another execution. You know, one of those weird "prophets." Claim they got the answer to all the world's problems. Bein' executed along with two other criminals.
	Calvinicus: Oh. He's the guy. Yeah, I heard about him. They say he's God or something. Some people say he did some kind of hocus-pocus on some sick people.
A small cross is carried in and set to one side.	*Georgius:* Yeah. These "prophets" are all the same. They supposedly fix a few legs and eyes, and everyone goes gaga. Course, he's also charged with creating a disturbance, inciting a riot, and contempt of court.

	They never learn. If he really wants a following, he's gotta explain how come his God is so good at fixing legs and so bad at gettin' him outta jail. Uh, look, I gotta get back to the house and start preparing for the feast tonight.
Calvinicus:	You know, George, just the other day I was telling the wife what a mess the world is in. On one hand, you got those radical Zealots and Essenes walking around with the short hair and stuff; on the other hand, you got those phony, loud-mouthed Pharisees running around blowing trumpets and prayin' in your ear. What are things coming to anyway?
Georgius:	I don't know, man. Why don't you ask Caesar?
Calvinicus:	I know this sounds weird, George, but sometimes I think if there is a God, I wish he'd do something radical about what's going on down here. I mean, you know, he could always come down here and zap a few Romans. Then maybe something would happen.
Georgius:	It'd be great if anything would happen around here! Every day, it's out to the fields—plow, plow, plow, grab a quick lunch, back to work, crunch the grain—the same old grind. What kind of life is that?
Calvinicus:	It would be great if we could all go back to the good old days of shepherding like the Waltonbergs.
Georgius:	Are you kidding? I wouldn't go back to sheep for nothin'. Progress, man, progress. Oh sure, it gets a little dusty in town with all the traffic, but this is where the action is. Of course, all this activity has made my wife nag a little more (if that's possible).
Calvinicus:	I don't know, man. Seems like I just wake up, turn off my rooster, go to work, go home, blow out the lamp, and go to bed. I wish there was something

A second small cross is brought in and set to the other side.

	more. I'm beginning to wonder about all this religious stuff. I mean, if there is such a thing as God, why doesn't he just come down here and say, "Hi, folks. I'm God. How'd you like to see a few Romans made into pizza."
Georgius:	You ought to know by now, Cal baby, religion is all a bunch of myths and stuff. Well, see you around.
A third large cross is slowly brought in.	
Calvinicus:	O.K., George, see you later.
Georgius:	*(sarcastically)* Yeah. By the way, Cal, if you bump into some guy that says, "Hi, I'm God," let me know. I'd like to meet him.

GIFTS OF BEAUTY

Here's a short skit that can be used as a start for discussion about the body of Christ or spiritual gifts (see 1 Cor. 12). Each participant in the skit should exaggerate his role and emphasize the part of the body that he is playing. For instance, the eyes could wear some giant glasses, and the mouth could use a megaphone. To increase the fun, label each part with a sign that is worn by the actors.

Feel free to add more lines or other parts of the body and create your own dialogue. Follow up with a discussion based on the subject matter presented.

Ear:	Where is Hand when I need him?
Eye:	He's over there picking Nose.
Ear:	What! He's always goofing off when I need him!
Mouth:	What do you need him for anyway?
Ear:	I need him to clean out the wax in me.
Hand:	I don't know why you guys are yelling at me. Look, Foot's in mouth!
Ear:	You both are a couple of goof-offs.
Eye:	To be honest, we've all been goofing off a lot lately.
Nose:	Yeah, look how bad we've made this kid we're on look.
Ear:	I heard the ugliest girl in town turned him down for a date.

Mouth:	Thank goodness! I'd hate to have to kiss *her* good night!
Feet:	Does anybody know how we can help him look better?
Eye:	I was reading the Bible the other day and it said that everyone has a spiritual gift. Maybe if we all find our spiritual gifts, we can make this kid look a lot better.
Everybody:	Yeah! Let's go!
Eye:	*(some length of time later)* Well, did everybody find their gifts?
Everybody:	Yeah!
Nose:	My gift is to smell all of the wonderful things God has made.
Eye:	My gift is to read the Scriptures and to see the good in others.
Ear:	My gift is to hear the sounds of nature and the voices of people.
Mouth:	My gift is to tell others about God.
Hand:	My gift is to help other people.
Feet:	My gift is to take us places where we can use our gifts.
Eye:	I'm sure glad I found my gift!
Nose:	Me, too! I was getting tired of running anyway.

GOD AND THE I.R.S.

This skit will generate some good discussion on the effectiveness of prayer. For best results, the actors *(four guys are needed)* should memorize their lines and perhaps insert recognizable names and places to make the situation more "local."

Scene One: A college frat house

Jim:	Hi, Mike. What's the matter? You look a little "down."
Mike:	Oh, hi Jim. Yeah, I'm down all right. Tomorrow's the deadline for paying my tuition, and I'm just not gonna be able to come up with the cash. So school's out for me, I guess. It's back to the salt mines.
Jim:	That's a shame. What about your folks? Can they help?
Mike:	No, not really. My dad's been out of work for the last couple of months, and they're gonna need whatever cash they have just to live on.
Jim:	Can you get a loan from somewhere?

Mike:	I've already tried. No luck. My credit's no good, my dad's credit's no good, and I still haven't paid off the last loan I managed to con the bank out of.
Jim:	How much do you need?
Mike:	$750.00—cash, check, or money order.
Jim:	Sheesh. That's a lot of dough. *(Bob enters.)*
Bob:	Hi, guys. What's new?
Mike:	750 bucks—that's what's new.
Bob:	Huh?
Jim:	He means if he doesn't come up with 750 bucks by tomorrow, it's back to washing dishes at Mabel's.
Bob:	Sorry to hear about it, Mike. Lucky for me, my old man has plenty of money. He just writes the school a check every year—no sweat.
Jim:	Yea, me too. Thank God for dads.
Mike:	Well, that's great for you, but what about me? What am I gonna do?
Bob:	Have you had much experience robbing banks?
Jim:	I hear there's big money in pushing drugs these days. *(laughs)*
Mike:	Come on, knock it off. This is serious. *(Pete enters.)* Hey, Peter, you got 750 bucks you wanna get rid of?
Pete:	Hi, Mike, hi, guys—750 bucks? What are you talking about? I couldn't afford a ticket to a free lunch.
Bob:	Mike needs money for school by tomorrow or his education comes to a screeching halt.
Pete:	A classic case of mal-tuition.
Mike:	Very funny. Ha ha. *(sarcastically)*
Pete:	I suppose you've already discussed trying to get a loan and so on.
Jim:	No good.
Pete:	Have you prayed about it?
Mike:	What? Get serious.
Pete:	I *am* serious. Have you prayed about it?
Bob:	Come on, man. What is God gonna do? Drop 750 dollars out of the sky by tomorrow?
Pete:	How should I know what God will do? But we *are* Christians, aren't we? We *are* supposed to have faith, you know.
Mike:	I think robbing a bank is easier.
Jim:	Look, Mike, it's worth a try. Jesus did say, "Ask and you will receive," didn't he?

Mike: But I'm not very good at praying, especially when I'm depressed.

Bob: Pete, why don't you pray? It was your idea.

Pete: O.K. by me. Let's pray right here. *(All four bow their heads, and Pete leads them in a prayer, which he can make up, asking God to help them solve Mike's money problems.)*

Mike: Thanks, Pete. Well, look, I better get going and see if I can find a money tree somewhere.

All: See you later. Good luck, Mike. Hope you find that tree.

Scene Two: The next day (Have someone hold up a card to that effect. Jim, Bob, and Mike meet again.)

Jim: Hey, Mike. You're looking a little better than you did yesterday. You must have found that money tree.

Mike: Hey, you're not going to believe what happened.

Bob: Good news, I hope.

Mike: After I left you guys yesterday, I went over to my folks' house, and there was an envelope addressed to me from the Internal Revenue Service. Inside it was a check for $774.13. I made a mistake on my taxes last year. They discovered it and refunded my money! What a stroke of luck! I just couldn't believe it!

Jim: Wow! God sure answered that prayer in a hurry!

Mike: God nothing, man. It was the I.R.S.! That check was in the mail way before Pete ever prayed. Thank you, Uncle Sam!

GROUNDED!

Here's a short skit that can generate good discussion about parents. It involves two characters, Tom and Scott, who meet after school with books in hand, to talk. *(Allow your actors to ad-lib these lines so that it sounds natural.)*

Tom: Hey, Scott, how about playing a little racquetball on Saturday? Judging from the last time we played, you could use a little work on your backhand!

Scott: Baloney! Last time I played with you I was just letting those backhand shots get by to let your confidence get built up. Next time, I won't be so nice.

Tom: Well, I'll let you redeem yourself on Saturday. What time?

Scott: Oh, wait a minute. I forgot. I've been grounded another week by my parents.

Tom: What? They are always on you for something. What is it this time? Did you rob a bank? Get busted with drugs? Or did you forget to put your napkin on your lap at the dinner table?

Scott: Actually, I got all B's on my report card.

Tom: You got grounded for getting B's on your report card?

Scott: Yeah, all B's, except for the C and two D's. My parents think I can do better. They're probably right, but, man, I really hate homework. Anyway, I'm grounded.

Tom: I can't believe your parents! I've *NEVER* gotten grounded. My parents don't even care what kind of grades I get. It's my business, not theirs.

Scott: Well, my folks aren't like that. They care about my grades. Obviously.

Tom: *(At this point, Tom and Scott turn toward the audience and talk as if they were just thinking.)* Boy, it must be rough to have parents who are on top of you all the time. But I'll have to say this about Scott's parents: They do love him and are concerned about him. Sometimes I wonder if my parents love me at all. I'd sure like to switch places with Scott for a week, just to feel that kind of love.

Scott: *(in thought)* It must be easy to get along with Tom's parents. They must have a lot of confidence in him to let him do whatever he wants. Sometimes I wonder if my parents will ever let me grow up. It must be nice never to be grounded. I'd love to trade places with Scott for a week or so.

Tom: *(still thinking)* No, it would never work. I'd feel boxed in. I need my freedom.

Scott: *(still thinking)* No, it would never work. My parents' love is too important to me.

Tom: Well, are you sure you can't talk your folks into letting you play racquetball on Saturday?

Scott: Nah, I'd love to play, but I better hit the books.

Tom: O.K., I'll just have to whip you again next time! See ya! *(They exit.)*

GROWING UP

Here is a skit that would be good for a Parents' Night Banquet. It requires eight people to perform "readers' theater" style. The readers should be seated on stage facing the audience. As with any good readers' theater, the lines should be rehearsed so that they don't *sound* like they are being read.

Feel free to change the dialogue and use the script only as a guide. Although no props are called for, you may use hats or other props to embellish the lines whenever appropriate.

#1:   Slap.

#2:   Waah.

#3:   Doctor, is it a girl?

#4:   Well, kinda.

#5:   Is it a boy?

#4:   Well, kinda.

#3:   We had twins? *(pause)*

#6:   Googoo, gaga.

#1:   What'd you name her?

#2:   Margaret Ethyl Beatrice Georgia Claire Elaine DeWitt

#1:   Oh. *(pause)*

#5:   Mama.

#3:   Open up little birdie, here comes Mama Birdie with some cream of meat loaf.

#4:   Pppppp . . . *(pause)*

#3:   Walkems to Dada.

#2:   Mommie! Mommie! Billy stoled my tricycle.

#1:   Hey, guys! Check out my new tooth!

All: Whoooo!

#6:   Mom, is Santa Claus for real?

#8:   No, silly, the Easter Bunny works overtime. *(pause)*

#5:   What you say is what you is!

#7:   Are!

#5:   What you are is what you is? *(pause)*

#8: But, baby-sitter! My Mommie and Daddie *always* lets us stay up later than that!

#2: (*singing*) Dis widdle light ob mine. I gonna let it shine. Dis widdle light ob mine. I gonna let it shine, let it shine— (*interrupted*)

#3: Eww, Cooties!

#2: Mommie, Timmy lifted up my dress! (*whining voice, pause*)

#4: Well, *my* mommie told me I could be anything I want to be.

#7: Well, what do you want to be?

#4: A brother.

#6: When I was little, I used to suck my thumb. (*pause*)

#8: Oh, look, Howard. It's our baby's first day in school.

#2: I don't like this dress, Mommie.

#1: Hey, Daddy, I got Mr. Smiley's Happy Kid Award.

#5: Now I lay me down to sleep, I pray the Lord my soul to keep. If I should die afore I wake, I pray the Lord, my soul to take. God bless Mommie, and Daddy, and everybody in the whole world. (*pause*)

#8: (*sing*) Ring around the rosies, pocketful of posies— (*interrupted*)

#3: Mary! Put that fish back in the bowl! (*pause*)

#4: Johnnie, whatcha writing?

#5: Nothing, none of your business.

#4: It's a love note, huh?

#5: No it's not! Now go to bed or I'm telling.

#4: (*giggles*) He keeps forgetting, I can read cursive now.

#1: Mom! Mom! I got chose hall monitor!

#3: Janet, look! I got the new Barbie Porsche.

All: Wow! (*pause*)

#5: `Hurry up, Sally. You're gonna miss the bus!

#7: Fire Cracker, Fire Cracker. Boom, Boom, Boom.

#2: Mark, truth or dare?

#6: Are you an early bird or a late bird?

#4: Eeeeeeeeeehhhh (*wicked witch laugh*)

#7: Mom, she's doing it again!

#8: Jenny, stop scaring your sister. (*pause*)

#6: (*singing*) I've got the Joy, Joy, Joy, Joy, down in my heart.

All:	Where?
#6:	Down in my heart . . .
All:	Where?
#6:	Down in my heart . . . *(fade out, pause)*
#7:	I just bought you new shoes two weeks ago.
#8:	Mom, you're the one who said I was a growing girl.
#3:	I can't believe you forgot my Little League game.
#2:	Get off my property! And stay out of my room!
#1:	Fatty, Fatty, two by four . . . *(pause)*
#7:	My mom will take us, if your mom will pick us up.
#6:	Mom, I hate the dentist.
#4:	You're the one with twelve cavities, Billy.
#6:	You should have bought Crest. *(pause)*
#1:	Hey, no cuts!
#2:	Wanna play handball?
#8:	Duck, duck, duck, duck, *(etc.)*
#5:	Say goose, already!
#8:	I was gonna. GOOSE! *(pause)*
#4:	Mom, no one wears this kind of dress on picture day. I look like Mary Poppins! *(pause)*
#7:	I'm only eating twelve peas.
#5:	I don't want to take piano lessons anymore.
#3:	One and, two and, three and, four and . . . *(practicing piano, pause)*
#1:	Clean up after the dog? But I have homework to do. *(pause)*
#2:	But all my friends wear makeup, Mom. This is the 80s.
#1:	Hey, Kevin, today's the big day.
#3:	Oh yeah, what's so big about it.
#1:	Today, I'm walking *her* home.
#3:	I don't think that's such a great idea.
#1:	Yeah? Why not?
#3:	Cause she's, uh, uh, a girl. *(pause)*
#7:	I'm gonna get a gunnysack for my eighth-grade graduation.
#5:	Big deal! I'm gonna get a skateboard.
All:	Freshman year

#2:   Hey! Check out these midget freshmen guys. *(pause)*

#4:   Honey, I promise, I'll just charge a little. They really do need some new school clothes.

#3:   She just went shopping last week. *(pause)*

#5:   Where do you buy tickets for the rally?

#6:   Right here my man, only $5.00 each.

#5: $5.00—what a bargain. *(pause)*

#8:   Sunday night! Oh no, I'm late again and *(name of music director)* is gonna kill me.

#2:   I have so much homework—can't go tonight. *(pause)*

#7:   Kathy, let's walk *AROUND* senior hall.

#4:   Teach, teacher, I'm lost.

All: Sophomore year

#1:   Hey, guys. Check it out. I got my license.

(CRASH)

#2:   Me, too, but my picture's gross. *(pause)*

#6:   Rad! I got a convertible!

#5:   Wow! I got a . . . Pinto!

Both #5:–#6: Let's take *YOUR/MY* Car. *(pause)*

#5:   Ring! Ring!

#3:   I'll get it— *(interrupted)*

#2:   No! I'll get it!

#4:   *(Yells)* I got it! *(pause)*

#7:   Youth choir practice? At 4:30 again?

#1:   Yes, and remember . . .

All: *(Together)* We know, be on time! *(pause)*

All: Junior year

#4:   TWO BITS, FOUR BITS, SIX BITS, A DOLLAR—ALL FOR *(your school)* STAND UP
        AND HOLLER. *(very loud, then pause)*

#2:   H'm, let's see, if I take Art 100 first period, I can take P.E. second period, then Typing
        200 third period, and Ping-Pong fourth period—

#4:   Oh, wait a minute. You promised to sign up for Flag Team.

#2:   There's no room left, and I forgot math and English. *(pause)*

#6:   Uh, Dad, could I, uh, like, use the car Friday night?

#5:   Well, sure, son.

#6:	Uh, Dad, could I, uh, borrow $10.00?
#5:	Well, I guess I can spare a little extra.
#6:	Uh, Dad, how about . . . ?
#5:	Don't press your luck, son. *(pause)*
#7:	I'll die if I have to wear that sweater again, I'll just die.
#4:	You have on entirely too much makeup. Now go wash your face. *(pause)*
#7:	It's too good to be true—a summer job—clothes, clothes, clothes . . .
#6:	You can't go? Oh, yeah, you have to work.
#7:	Guess who just asked me to the prom?
All:	Blaze Warner *(name of popular guy)* OHHHHHHHH! *(pause)*
All:	Senior Year
#1:	Hello, uh, *(cough)* there's this party this weekend. Would you, like I mean, would you like to go?
#5:	Um, h'm.
#1:	Oh? *(surprised)* You would? Oh, well, that's great!
#5:	Well, I'll talk to you later.
#1:	I can't believe I finally have a date. *(pause)*
#3:	Four credits! How could I be missing four credits?
#2:	The SAT test . . . all day long?
#8:	I'm not ready for this. *(pause)*
#4:	Why are you wearing those ridiculous sunglasses in your senior picture?
#1:	Sunglasses? Those are my NETS. (NAYS) *(pause)*
All:	*(to the tune of "Pomp and Circumstance")* Da, da, da, da, da . . . da.
#6:	Eighteen, where has the time gone?
#2:	They're growing up. *(pause)*
All:	(Make up some words to a familiar tune and sing to the parents.)

THE GUEST

Here is a short Christmas play that is an adaptation of the poem "How the Great Guest Came" by Edwin Markham. While the original poem's setting was in Europe a few centuries ago, the setting for this version of the story is the present.

THE GUEST

Characters:

Conrad	The Woman	Two passers-by
Ellspith	The Old Man	Narrator
Barclay	The Kid	

Props:

street lamp	bread	chairs or sofa
fireplace	milk	lamp
table	honey	other furnishings
bookshelf	door	costumes
shoes		

THE GUEST

Narrator: Before the cathedral in grandeur rose
At Ingelburg where the Danube goes;
Before its forest of silver spires
Went airily up to the clouds and fires:
Before the oak had ready a beam,
While yet the arch was stone and dream—
There where the altar was later laid,
Conrad, the cobbler, plied his trade.

Ellspith: *(knock, knock)*

Conrad: Bark! Bark!

Ellspith: *(knock, knock)*

Conrad: *(as he walks to the door)* Bark! Bark! Down, Fang! Bark! Bark! Quiet. Bark! *(growls and opens the door)* Hello, Ellspith! Merry Christmas! Come in, come in.

Ellspith: Conrad, old friend. A Merry Christmas to you, too. Conrad, what was barking? You don't have a watchdog.

Conrad:	I know. I can't afford one. So when someone comes to the door, I have to bark myself.
Ellspith:	Oh, Conrad, we are all feeling the financial pinch.
Conrad:	Where's Barclay?
Ellspith:	He's coming any minute.
Barclay:	*(knock, knock)*
Ellspith:	That's him now.
Barclay:	*(knock, knock)*
Ellspith:	Who's there?
Barclay:	Snue!
Ellspith:	Snue! *(opens door)* What's Snue?
Barclay:	I don't know. What's Snue with you? Say, Conrad old boy, did you fix my sole?
Conrad:	Only the Lord can fix your soul, Barclay. But I did fix your shoe. *(hands him shoe and taps on the sole)*
Barclay:	How delightful. Now I have my Christmas shoes to wear with my Christmas stockings. They were knit by my dear, dear aunt. Do you know what they call my aunt, Conrad?
Conrad:	Probably Marnie Farnstock. That was her name.
Barclay:	*(exasperated)* I mean after she died.
Conrad:	They called her the late Marnie Farnstock.
Barclay:	They called her Marner the Darner. She used to say, "The hand that darns the sock . . ."
Ellspith:	". . . is usually the one that socks the husband!" Come, Barclay. We have to get you home into your socks. *(They start to leave.)*
Conrad:	Ellspith. Barclay.
Ellspith:	Yes, Conrad.
Conrad:	Before you leave, I must share my heart with you.
Ellspith:	Conrad, please do.
Barclay:	Yes, we *are* your friends.
Conrad:	*(dramatically, gazing heavenward)* At dawn today As night slipped away . . . The Lord appeared in a dream to me

And said, "I am coming your Guest to be!"
So I've been busy with feet astir,
Strewing the floor with branches of fir.
The wall is washed and the shelf is shined,
And over the rafter the holly twined.
He comes today, and the table is spread
With milk and honey and wheaten bread.

Ellspith: *(staring blank-faced straight at Conrad)* Why is he talking in poetry?

Barclay: Too much Lutefish, I suspect.

Ellspith: Listen, Conrad. It's Christmas and your thoughts are filled with Christ's coming. No doubt your dreams merely reflected what you have been thinking all day.

Barclay: Ellspith's right, Conrad. I mean, Christ's not really going to come to your door.

Conrad: *(pause)* Perhaps you are right. That *is* a little unusual. But it seemed so real.

Ellspith: We have to go, old friend, have a delightful Christmas.

Barclay: And if Jesus does come, send for us. We wise and royal beings will come, bearing our gifts of mirth and frankenstein. *(Ellspith pulls Barclay out through the door by scarf.)*

(appropriate farewells)

POOR WOMAN

Woman: *(Conrad sees a woman shivering in the cold, selling coal to passers-by. He invites her into his home to warm herself.)* Thank you kindly, sir. The weather is miserable out there.

Conrad: It certainly is foggy.

Woman: The visibility is so bad even the birds are walking. *(She sneezes right in his face.)*

Conrad: *(slightly put off, but polite)* Excuse me, ma'am, but could you sneeze the other way?

Woman: I don't know no other way.

Conrad: Here. Sit down by the fire and warm yourself. Tell me how you came to such a wretched condition!

Woman: I was raised in poverty. We had nothing when I was growing up. And then . . . and then I met John. He was rich. Sophisticated. He was the only banker unaffected by the crash of '29.

Conrad:	Really?
Woman:	He went broke in '28. Ever since then we lived in a dreary apartment in town. Our furniture was meager and shabby. We had one little worn rug on our cold floor. It looked so bad my mother would say, "That rug looks terrible. Sweep it under the dirt!"
Conrad:	What does your husband do now?
Woman:	Oh, he passed away last year. I told him that if he were to die, starvation would stare me in the face. He said, "Doesn't sound pleasant for either of you!" So now it is just me and my children.
Conrad:	Woman, how can I help you?
Woman:	You dear man. You can't help. *(gets up to go to the door)* I can see that you are not much better off than I. I am simply trying to sell some coal to purchase some fresh milk and bread for my family.
Conrad:	*(turns and looks at the table)* Here, take this.
Woman:	*(awed by this great sacrifice)* God bless you, my friend.
Conrad:	Merry Christmas.

THE OLD MAN

Man:	*(knock, knock)*
Conrad:	Bark! Bark! Ah! It'll never work! I just don't sound enough like a dog. Coming! *(He opens the door. Man throws a bone in.)* What's that for?
Man:	I thought I heard a dog.
Conrad:	Ah, yes. He passed away. I just laid him to rest. What can I do for you, old man?
Man:	I am receiving Christmas donations for the Buford T. Ellis Memorial Fund.
Conrad:	And who, may I ask, is Buford T. Ellis?
Man:	At your service, Sir. *(bows dramatically with top hat)*
Conrad:	*(chuckling)* Come in, old-timer, you look like you could use at least a rest.
Man:	Thank you, Sir. Usually I am not received in such kindness.
Conrad:	It's the least I can do. Here, sit down.
Man:	*(sits down, puts feet up on little table, and pulls out stogy)*
Conrad:	So you are collecting money?
Man:	I am. I need some extra bucks for my expensive hobby.

Conrad:	And what hobby is that?
Man:	Eating.
Conrad:	You know it would be nice to have a lot of money. But really, money only brings misery.
Man:	But with money you can afford to be miserable. This Thanksgiving I asked myself, "What do I have to be thankful for? I can't even pay my bills."
Conrad:	Be thankful you're not one of your creditors.
Man:	That's true. You know, I used to get by fairly well with my small business. But I have suffered one financial disaster after another.
Conrad:	It's been a tough life for you, hasn't it?
Man:	It hasn't been easy, but God has helped me.
Conrad:	Listen, old man. I don't have much. But here, take these shoes. You could stand a new pair.
Man:	(looking very happy) You are very generous. (He rips off his old shoes, and they fall apart, so he puts on new ones.) They fit perfectly! Thank you, Sir. (He leaves. They exchange farewells.)

THE KID

Kid:	(knock, knock)
Conrad:	(opens door)
Kid:	(sings) While shepherds washed their socks by night, all seated on the ground—
Conrad:	(interrupts) Hold it! Hold it! I think you have some of the words mixed up there. It's "watched," not "washed."
Kid:	While shepherds watched their socks by night—
Conrad:	Wait! And it's "flocks," not "socks."
Kid:	What are flocks?
Conrad:	They're a bunch of sheep. Do you know what sheep are? (Kid shakes head no.) They're little woolly things, kind of like socks! Merry Christmas! What can I do for you on this blessed day?
Kid:	I'm collecting arms for the poor.
Conrad:	That's "alms."
Kid:	What are alms?

Conrad:	They're gifts, usually money.
Kid:	OH NO!
Conrad:	What's the problem?
Kid:	I've been going through the streets crying, "Arms for the poor, arms for the poor!"
Conrad:	Land o' Goshen! And what did you get?
Kid:	Strange looks. I'll *never* get any money.
Conrad:	Who are the poor you're collecting for?
Kid:	_____ (pastor's name) Home for Wayward Children.
Conrad:	There's no home there.
Kid:	Well, there's the Agony General Hospital, too.
Conrad:	Never heard of it.
Kid:	Would you believe the Shuffleboard Retirement Center?
Conrad:	(shakes head) Why don't you just tell me where the money is really going?
Kid:	(face down, ashamed of his poverty) It's for me.
Conrad:	That's what I thought. It looks like you need it.
Kid:	But it's not really for me. It's for my sister. I want to give her a present this Christmas. We don't have very much, and, well, I love my little sister . . . I thought I might give her something special.
Conrad:	(looks at the table, gives the kid the honey)
Kid:	(looks inside) Wow! Is this real honey?
Conrad:	Yes, give it to your sister. And here, give her these shoes, and here is a pair for you.
Kid:	Wow! You are something, Mister. Thank you. (excitedly leaves)
Conrad:	(as he leaves) Hey, lad! What is your sister going to give you for Christmas?
Kid:	I don't know. Last year she gave me the measles! Bye, Mister!
Conrad:	Merry Christmas!

(While the narrator reads, Conrad wanders around room looking sad, but as he realizes that Christ came to him in those three people, he begins to look radiant.)

Narrator:	The day went down in the crimson west
	And with it the hope of the blessed Guest,
	And Conrad sighed as the world turned gray:
	"Why is it, Lord, that your feet delay?

Did You forget that this was the day?"
Then soft in the silence a Voice he heard:
"Lift up your heart, for I kept my word.
Three times I came to your friendly door;
Three times my shadow was on your floor.
I was the beggar with bruised feet;
I was the woman you gave food to eat;
I was the child on the homeless street!"

HE'S GOING TO WHAT?

The following dialogue makes a great short Christmas play for two people. Be creative with props, costumes, or whatever. Be sure your actors memorize their lines and rehearse. During the advent season, this story is also effective as a reading or as a discussion-starter.

Angel #1: He's going down himself.

Angel #2: What?

Angel #1: I said, he's going down!

Angel #2: Who told you?

Angel #1: This morning during devotions he called Michael and Gabriel up and began to tell them, in front of us all, about The Plan.

Angel #2: Why do I always miss the good parts?

Angel #1: Where were you?

Angel #2: Bythnia; I had to help little Lydia across that icy bridge again. But do go on. What is The Plan?

Angel #1: It has to do with the prophets' predictions.

Angel #2: So! The Day of the Lord is finally here. I guess I wasted my time helping Lydia. If he's bringing it all to a close now, she'll be up here with us soon anyway.

Angel #1: It's not that simple. He's planning to straighten out the situation down there.

Angel #2: Well, why doesn't he send Moses? Or Elijah? Or Gabriel?

Angel #1: He will—each at their appointed time. But, they can only take a message. I did hear that Gabriel is to arrange the entrance preparations.

Angel #2: Oh, wow! I can see it now—all those humans wandering about in their busyness when all of a sudden the sun, stars, and sky roll back. Then out of the deepness of eternity, he steps foot on their planet. I wish I could be there to see their faces. How about old Augustus? He'll fall right off his pedestal.

Angel #1: It's not going to be that way. He doesn't even plan to show up at Rome.

Angel #2: No Rome? So! He's going to Jerusalem. Imagine—the high priest will look up and suddenly there he is. Won't that wrinkle his robe!

Angel #1: I doubt that will happen.

Angel #2: Oh? Don't tell me he won't see the high priest.

Angel #1: Yes, he will see the high priest and all his council, but I doubt if they will recognize him.

Angel #2: Not recognize the Lord of Glory? Does he plan to disguise himself?

Angel #1: In a way . . .

Angel #2: Why doesn't he want them to know who he is?

Angel #1: The way I understand it, he wants them to recognize him by his life and his works, not by his appearance.

Angel #2: I'm assuming he'll go as a man, a Jewish man no doubt.

Angel #1: I hear he's planning his entry as a baby.

Angel #2: A what?

Angel #1: A baby, a humanette.

Angel #2: Incredible! But . . . but isn't he taking a big chance? The security will be fantastic. Why, we'll have to form a couple myriads of bodyguards twenty-four hours a day.

Angel #1: He's going to be on his own.

Angel #2: And turn him loose with that pack of "crazies"?

Angel #1: Do you honestly think there's any way they can harm him against his will?

Angel #2: Of course, you're right. He'll be taking his power with him. Can't you see the little tyke lying there in his mother's arms one minute, then jumping up the next to give a Roman soldier a karate chop?

Angel #1: I've heard his power will only be used to help others. He doesn't think it necessary to show all his credentials. And he already has the mother picked out.

Angel #2: I hope it's not Lydia's mother.

Angel #1: Who?

Angel #2: Lydia, the little girl from Bythnia. Imagine letting your four-year-old walk across a slick bridge like that. Anyway, I suppose he's picked out a priest's family or a family of the Pharisees.

Angel #1: No, she's a poor, young unknown by the name of Mary. And, now keep this quiet, I wouldn't want every angel in the galaxy to hear this. He's going to be born in a stall, a cattle stable, right in the stench of earthly hay and stubble.

Angel #2: But, that's criminal! It can't be! I won't allow it! I protest!

Angel #1: To whom?

Angel #2: I just don't understand the purpose in all this.

Angel #1: You know as well as I do how he loves them. Now, listen, here's where we fit in. He does want us to line up a few witnesses to record the event for future generations.

Angel #2: Sure, I've got it. How about 1,000 men from each of the twelve tribes of Israel?

Angel #1: I said just a few.

Angel #2: How about 100 each . . . ?

Angel #1: No. He wants only a few.

Angel #2: Well, how about a couple scribes, a lawyer, a politician, and a news reporter, of course.

Angel #1: That definitely won't do. Besides, he has them picked out already. Here's the list.

Angel #2: Let's see. Three astrologers from Arbela? Where's that?

Angel #1: Over on the east side of the Tigris.

Angel #2: But they're foreigners, outsiders.

Angel #1: Don't forget the others, too.

Angel #2: Oh, yes, there's Jason, Demas, and Hakiah. Who are they?

Angel #1: Shepherds, I believe.

Angel #2: Just common, ordinary hillside shepherds?

Angel #1: It's his style, you know. Look at Abraham. What was he? And David? And what was Moses doing out there when the bush caught on fire?

Angel #2: I see what you mean.

Angel #1: One thing does bother me, though. Who down there will believe the shepherds?

Angel #2: Lydia would.

Angel #1: Yes, I love those humanettes. They believe whatever we tell them.

Angel #2: They do until Satan gets ahold of them. By the way, what will he be doing all this time? He won't like this one bit.

Angel #1: I figure he'll try to incite the humans to hateful and brutal actions.

Angel #2: You don't suppose they'll keep falling for his old lines, do you?

Angel #1: They're like putty in his hands most of the time. But, I do hear that our Lord will pull off some pretty big miracles, and then, there's The Final Presentation.

Angel #2: When's that?

Angel #1: I don't know for sure. It's top secret.

Angel #2: I see. Well, now, let me review. All we have to do is go down, talk to the shepherds, and come back here and watch him do the rest. Right?

Angel #1: Right. There's the preliminary signal. It's just about time for us to go down.

Angel #2: Wow! What a day. I thought I wouldn't have anything to do until the bridge freezes over again.

Angel #1: Remember, only a few shepherds. And please don't scare them.

Angel #2:   I promise, I promise.

Angel #1:   There's the signal. Let's go.

Angel #2:   Do you think we could stop by Bythnia on the way back? It's about time for Lydia to say her prayers. I just love the way she prays.

Angel #1:   Oh, I guess so. Now, hurry.

Angel #2:   I'm right behind you. But, I was wondering, what if it doesn't work out the way we think? What if there's a lot of resistance to The Plan? Down there as a vulnerable human, why, he could get himself killed!

Angel #1:   Don't be ridiculous!

Narrator: And there were shepherds living out in the fields nearby, keeping watch over their flocks at night. An angel of the Lord appeared to them, and the glory of the Lord shone around them, and they were terrified. But the angel said to them, "Do not be afraid. I bring you good news of great joy that will be for all the people. Today in the town of David a Savior has been born to you; he is Christ the Lord. This will be a sign to you: You will find a baby wrapped in cloths and lying in a manger." Suddenly a great company of the heavenly host appeared with the angel, praising God and saying, "Glory to God in the highest, and on earth peace to men on whom his favor rests" (Luke 2:8–14).

IF GOD SHOULD SPEAK

This skit deals with prayer and other issues of the Christian life. It requires one person who is the "pray-er" and someone else who is the voice of God, offstage.

Pray-er: "Our Father which art in heaven . . ."

God: Yes.

Pray-er: Don't interrupt me. I'm praying.

God: But you called me.

Pray-er: Called you? I didn't call you. I'm praying. "Our Father which art in heaven . . ."

God: There, you did it again.

Pray-er: Did what?

God:	Called me. You said, "Our Father which art in heaven." Here I am. What's on your mind?
Pray-er:	But I didn't mean anything by it. I was, you know, just saying my prayers for the day. I always say the Lord's Prayer. It makes me feel good, you know, kind of like getting a duty done.
God:	All right. Go on!
Pray-er:	"Hallowed be thy name . . ."
God:	Hold it! What do you mean by that?
Pray-er:	By what?
God:	By "Hallowed be thy name?"
Pray-er:	It means . . . it means . . . Good grief! I don't know what it means! How should I know? It's just part of the prayer. By the way, what does it mean?
God:	It means honored, holy, wonderful.
Pray-er:	Hey, that makes sense. I never thought what "hallowed" meant before. "Thy kingdom come, thy will be done, on earth as it is in heaven."
God:	Do you really mean that?
Pray-er:	Sure, why not?
God:	What are you doing about it?
Pray-er:	Doing? Nothing, I guess. I just think it would be kind of neat if you got control of everything down here like you have up there.
God:	Have I got control of you?
Pray-er:	Well, I go to church.
God:	That isn't what I asked you. What about that habit of lying you have? And your temper? You've really got a problem there, you know. And then there's the way you spend your money—all on yourself. And what about the kinds of books you read?
Pray-er:	Stop picking on me! I'm just as good as some of the rest of those people—those phonies—at church!
God:	Excuse me! I thought you were praying for my will to be done. If that is to happen, it will have to start with the ones who are praying for it. Like you, for example.
Pray-er:	Oh, all right. I guess I do have some problems, some hang-ups. Now that you mention it, I could probably name some others.
God:	So could I.

Pray-er:	I haven't thought about it very much until now, but I really would like to cut out some of those things. I would like to, you know, be really free.
God:	Good! Now we are getting somewhere. We'll work together, you and I. Some victories can truly be won. I'm proud of you!
Pray-er:	Look, Lord! I need to finish up here. This is taking a lot longer than it usually does. "Give us this day, our daily bread."
God:	You need to cut out some of that "bread." You're overweight as it is.
Pray-er:	Hey, wait a minute! What is this, Criticize-Me Day? Here I was, doing my religious duty, and all of a sudden you break in and remind me of all my problems and shortcomings.
God:	Praying is a dangerous thing. You could wind up changed, you know. That's what I'm trying to get across to you. You called me, and here I am. It's too late to stop now. Keep on praying. I'm interested in the next part of your prayer. *(pause)* Well, go on!
Pray-er:	I'm afraid to.
God:	Afraid? Afraid of what?
Pray-er:	I know what you'll say next.
God:	Try me and see.
Pray-er:	"Forgive us our trespasses, as we forgive those who trespass against us."
God:	What about Joe?
Pray-er:	I knew it! See, I knew you would bring him up! Why, Lord, he's told lies about me, and cheated me out of some money, and is the biggest phoney around. He never paid back that debt he owes me. I've sworn to get even with him and then never associate with him again!
God:	But your prayer! What about your prayer?
Pray-er:	I didn't mean it.
God:	Well, at least you're honest. But it's not much fun carrying that load of bitterness around inside you, is it?
Pray-er:	No, but I'll feel better as soon as I get even. Boy, have I got some plans for old Joe! He'll wish he never did me any harm.
God:	You won't feel any better. You'll only feel worse. Revenge isn't sweet. Think of how unhappy you are already. But I can change all that.
Pray-er:	You can? How?

God:	Forgive Joe. Then the hate and sin will be Joe's problem, not yours. You may lose the money, but you will have settled your heart.
Pray-er:	But Lord, I can't forgive Joe.
God:	Then, how do you expect me to forgive you?
Pray-er:	Oh, you're right! You always are! And more than I want revenge on Joe, I need to be right with you. All right, I forgive him. Lord, you help him to find the right road in life. He's bound to be awfully miserable now that I think about it. Anybody who goes around doing the things he does has to be out of it. Some way, somehow, show him the right way. Maybe you can even help me to help him?
God:	There now! Wonderful! How do you feel?
Pray-er:	H'm! Well, not bad. Not bad at all. In fact, I feel pretty great! You know, I don't think I'll have to go to bed uptight tonight for the first time since I can remember. Maybe I won't be so tired from now on because I'm not getting enough rest.
God:	You're not through with your prayer. Go on!
Pray-er:	Oh, all right. "And lead us not into temptation, but deliver us from evil."
God:	Good! Good! I'll do that. Just don't put yourself in a place where you can be tempted.
Pray-er:	What do you mean by that?
God:	Change some of your friendships. Some of your so-called friends are beginning to get to you. Don't be fooled! They advertise that they're having fun, but for you it could be ruin. Either you are going to have to stop being with them or start being a positive influence on their lives. Don't you use me as an escape hatch!
Pray-er:	I don't understand.
God:	Sure you do. You've done it a lot of times. You get caught in a bad situation. You get into trouble by not listening to me, and then once you do, you come running to me, saying, "Lord, help me out of this mess, and I promise you I'll never do it again." You remember some of those bargains you tried to make with me, don't you?
Pray-er:	Yes I do, and I'm ashamed, Lord. I really am.
God:	Which bargain are you remembering?
Pray-er:	Well, when the woman next door saw me coming out of that X-rated movie with my friends. I'd told my mother we were going to the mall. I remember telling you, "Oh, God, don't let her tell my mother where I've been." I promised to be in church every Sunday.

God:	She didn't tell your mother, but you didn't keep your promise, did you?
Pray-er:	I'm sorry, Lord, I really am. Up until now, I thought that if I just prayed the Lord's Prayer every day, then I could do what I liked. I didn't expect anything like this to happen.
God:	Go ahead and finish your prayer!
Pray-er:	"For thine is the kingdom, and the power, and the glory, for ever. Amen."
God:	Do you know what would bring me glory? What would make me really happy?
Pray-er:	No, but I'd like to know. I want to please you. I know what a difference it can make in my life. I can see what a mess I've made of my life, and I can see how great it would be to be really one of your followers.
God:	You just answered my question.
Pray-er:	I did?
God:	Yes. The thing that would bring me glory is to have people like you truly love me. And I see that happening between us now. Now that these old sins are exposed and out of the way, well, there's no telling what we can do together.
Pray-er:	Lord, let's see what we can make of me and my life, O.K.?
God:	Yes, let's see!

Reprinted and adapted from *If God Talked Out Loud* by Clyde Lee Herring, ch. 1. © Copyright 1977, Broadman Press. All rights reserved. Used by permission.

THE INNKEEPER'S WIFE

This one-person monologue makes an excellent discussion-starter at Christmastime. The lines should be memorized, and a few props would be helpful. Use your own imagination and change or add any lines that you feel would improve the impact of delivery. The discussion could center around how we often are like the innkeeper's wife, missing opportunities in our lives to be of service to Christ.

Innkeeper's wife:	(*Lady comes in with cleaning rag and apron, muttering to herself as she begins to clean.*)

I'm so tired of all this cleaning! Seems like all I ever do! *(Phone begins to ring.)* I'll *never* get finished if this phone doesn't stop ringing. *(She answers phone.)* Hello, Bethlehem Inn, may I help you? Oh, hi, Mable. *Terrible.* Just terrible! Hardly got any sleep last night! Why? You mean you haven't heard? Well, you know Caesar has passed this *amendment* about taxing! I just don't understand this government—it's such a mess! That's right. Because of all this, so many folks have been traveling—we've just been *packed!* You should see the parking lot—it's *full* of camels and donkeys! And you know what a *mess* they make! Yes, David has been sick and the girls gave up their room to some travelers. Why, we even had folks sleeping in the hall last night, and you know what a fire hazard *that* is!

Well, Joe had to cut some more wood, so I had to get all the kids in bed and check in the guests. Got 'em all to bed, fixed Joe some supper, and *finally* got to bed myself! *Yeah,* uh-huh. Along about two o'clock there was this *loud banging* on the door! I nearly flew out of the bed with heart flutters! Oh, goodness me! That was so *frightening.* Uh-huh. So Joe goes down to the door and I peeped out the window. Couldn't believe what I saw! There was a young couple on a donkey and she was *pregnant!* Yes, uh-huh, *real* far along! And out in that cold, too! I heard it got down to ten below here in Bethlehem last night. *NO!* We didn't have a choice! Every room was packed! They said that every inn for the past two miles had been full, too.

Yeah. Well, Joe gave them the key to the barn, so they could at least get out of that wind, and she looked like she could have had that baby any minute! Uh-huh, uh-huh. By that time the kids were awake and fighting over the pillows—*Man,* did I need an *Alka Seltzer!* Uh-huh!

Just *barely* got back to sleep and heard some more noise outside. Looked out the window and saw *more camels!* People looked kinda like shepherds—I figured they could just find their way back to the barn, too. Yeah. *(starts to look at her watch)* Uh-huh, uh-huh.

Who? Oh, yeah, she had the baby all right. I found out this morning. A king after Caesar? Sure, Mabel, you've really lost it this time! I'm sure a king is going to be born in a barn. Well, I don't care *who* it is! I'm not going down there to help after all the trouble they've caused *me!* I'll just be glad when they're *gone. What?* Mable, I'm *sorry!* We just didn't *have room! (looks at watch)* I just don't have time! I've got lots to do here. I'll probably be the one who has to clean up all this camel mess! *Yuk!* Yeah, uh-huh, I gotta go! Bye! *(hangs up and mutters)* Some people just don't understand! I've got work to do! *(exit)*

THE JERK

Here's a skit that combines great humor with a clear message about conformity, peer pressure, and the values of the world.

Characters: Three guys (1, 2, 3); The "Jerk" (4)

1:        *(1, 2, 3 enter wearing party hats on their knees. They are laughing and joking.)* She called him a jerk right in front of the whole class! *(All laugh.)* Then Mrs. Higginbottom walks in—you should have seen her face when she saw Bobby standing on her desk.

2:     I heard she cussed him out and then he cussed her out.

1:     Nah, but I bet she wanted to. She sure yelled at him. Then she kicked him out of class for two weeks.

3:     Bobby deserves whatever happens to him. He *is* a real jerk.

2:     Speaking of jerks—look who's coming.

4:     *(enters wearing a party hat on his head)* Hi, guys. What's up?

3:     Nothin' much, _____ *(4's name)*. What are you up to?

4:     Just on my way to basketball practice.

2:     *(low voice to 1 and 3)* What's the deal with this guy wearing that thing on his head?

1:     *(low voice)* I don't know, but it looks about as nerdish as you can get. Gag!

4:     So, you guys comin' to the game tomorrow night?

1, 2, 3: *(shrugging)* Maybe. *(or)* I don't know.

1:     Hey, _____ *(4's name)*, do you play ball with that *(pointing to 4's hat)* on your head?

4:     Nah, it gets in the way and falls off.

2:     Why do you wear a knee cap on your head anyway?

4:     A what?

2:     A knee cap. Like these. *(pointing to the party hat on his knee)*

4:     Oh, well, I just thought that's the place you're supposed to wear it. I thought it was a hat.

3:     A hat? *(1, 2, and 3 laugh.)*

2:     You're kidding, right?

4:     No, I've always been taught by my parents that you wear this on your head.

1:     Who are you gonna believe? Your parents or us? We're your friends, aren't we? We wouldn't lead you astray.

2:     It's just that wearing a knee cap on your head looks kind of . . . kind of weird. Everybody wears them on their knees.

4:     Not everybody. I know a lot of people that call these hats and wear them on their heads.

1:     Can't be anybody we know.

2:     At least nobody important. Who are they?

4:     People at my church. They all—

2:     *(interrupting)* That figures.

4:	What?
2:	The same kind of people that go to church wear knee caps on their heads. That shows how weird religious people can be.
4:	Speaking of weird—have you guys looked at your knees in the mirror lately? I think wearing party hats on your knees is extra weird.
3:	Why do you always have to be different, _____ (4's name)? I mean, since you became a Christian, you don't act like everyone else anymore.
4:	What's wrong with being different?
2:	Nothing. It's just the things you choose to do different. Stuff that really gags us, you know?
1:	There are some things you just gotta do if you want to be part of the crowd.
4:	I don't understand why I can't just be myself. Why do I have to imitate everyone around me? If I'm going to imitate anyone, I should imitate the perfect model, Jesus. *(pause)* I better get going. I'll be late. *(exits then steps back in)* By the way, Jesus wore a knee cap on his head, too. *(exits)*
2:	Big deal. Mr. Religion has to spout off about his friend, Mr. Jesus. He's a class one jerk.
3:	But he did have a good point—about it being O.K. to be different, to be yourself.
2:	The only point he has is on his head. Come on, let's get out of here.
3:	You guys go ahead. There's something I gotta do. I'll catch up with you later. *(1 and 2 exit. 3 looks cautiously around, glances down at his party hats, thinks a moment, then decides to take one hat off and put it on his head.)*
1:	*(from offstage)* Hey, _____ 3's name, you comin' or not?
3:	Yeah, just a second. *(adjusting hat, getting the feel of it, saying to 1)* You know, there's something I've been thinking about.
1:	*(stepping on stage with a party hat on his head)* Yeah? What is it?
3:	*(looks at 1, pausing)* Uh, never mind, it's nothin'.

JESUS MET A WOMAN

Scripture readings come alive when the text is prepared in script form as in the following example. Many of the narrative sections of both Old and New Testaments may be adapted for group use with excellent results. Assign parts, have a reading, and then discuss the content of this skit, based on John 4.

Characters: Narrator
               Jesus
               Woman
               Disciple

Narrator: Jesus was journeying northward from Judea to Galilee and he had to pass through Samaria on the way. It was located near the village of Sychar on the piece of property that Jacob had given to his son Joseph. Tired from the long walk in the hot sun, Jesus sat down beside a well while his disciples went into the village to buy food. A Samaritan woman came to the well to draw water.

Jesus: Would you give me a drink of water?

Woman: You are a Jew and I am a Samaritan—how can you ask me for a drink?

Narrator: The Jews usually would not even speak to Samaritans, much less drink from the same cup.

Jesus: If you only knew what a wonderful gift God could give you and who I am, you would ask me for some living water.

Woman: But you don't even have a bucket and this is a deep well. Where would you get living water? Besides, you surely are not greater than our ancestor Jacob. How can you offer better water than this, which he and his family and his cattle drank?

Jesus: Everyone who drinks the water from this well will become thirsty again, but whoever drinks the water I will give him will never be thirsty again. For my gift will become a spring within him which will provide him with living water and give him eternal life.

Woman: Please, Sir, give me some of that water! Then I'll never be thirsty again and won't have to make this long trip out here to draw water.

Jesus: Go, get your husband, and then come back here.

Woman: But, I'm not married.

Jesus: You are telling the truth when you say you are not married. You have been married to five men, and the man you are living with now is not really your husband.

Woman: You must be a prophet, Sir! But, if I may ask a question, why do you Jews insist that Jerusalem is the only place of worship. We Samaritans, meanwhile, claim it is where our ancestors worshiped here at Mount Gerizim.

Jesus: Believe me, ma'am, the time is coming when we will no longer be concerned about the place to worship the Father! For it's not where we worship that's important, but how we worship. Worship must be spiritual and real, for God is Spirit and we must have his Spirit's help to worship as we should. The Father wants this kind of worship. But you Samaritans know so little about him, worshiping with your eyes shut, so to speak. We Jews know all about him, for salvation comes to mankind through the Jewish race.

Woman: Well, at least I know that the Messiah will come—you know, the one they call Christ—and when he does, he will make everything plain to us.

Jesus: I am the Messiah!

Narrator: Then the woman left her water pot beside the well, went back to the village, and excitedly told everyone about Jesus. Soon the people came streaming from the village to see him. In the meantime, the disciples had returned to Jesus. They had seen him talking to the Samaritan woman and were astonished, but they did not ask Jesus why, nor what he had said to the woman. Instead they urged Jesus to eat.

Disciple: Teacher, eat some of the food we bought.

Jesus: No. I have some food you don't know about.

Disciple: (to other disciples) Did someone else bring him food?

Jesus: My nourishment comes from doing the will of God who sent me and from finishing his work. Do you think the work of harvesting will not begin until the summer ends, four months from now? Open your eyes and look around you! Fields of human souls are ripening all around us, and they are ready for harvesting. The reaper of the harvest is being paid now and he gathers the crops for eternal life; the planter and the reaper will be glad together, for in this harvest the old saying comes true: "One man plants and another reaps." I have sent you to harvest a crop in a field where you did not labor; others labored there and you profit from their work.

Narrator: Many of the Samaritans in that town believed in Jesus because the woman had told them of his ability to know all things. So when the Samaritans came to him, they begged him to stay with them and Jesus stayed there two days. Many more believed because of Jesus' own words, and the villagers told the woman: "We believe now, not because of what you said, but because we have heard him with our own ears, and we know that he is the Savior of the world."

SAMPLE DISCUSSION QUESTIONS

1. Discuss the woman's growing conception of who Jesus was. Who do you think Jesus was?
2. Compare and contrast Jesus' attitude, the disciples' attitude, and the typical Jewish attitude toward this woman of another race.
3. What is the living water of which Jesus spoke?
4. What did Jesus teach the woman about worship?
5. Discuss the nature of the harvest Jesus spoke about.
6. If you took the teachings of this passage seriously, what specific differences could there be in your life tomorrow?

JOHN THE READY

A good skit about John the Baptist, be sure and follow it up with a discussion on the issues raised.

Characters needed: Narrator
John
A Questioner
Tax Collector
Soldier
Priest 1
Priest 2

Narrator: There was a man who was sent from God named John.
John: I am John.
Narrator: John was the Light.
John: That's what some people thought, but I only came to show the light.
Narrator: Sorry about that, John. Anyway John baptized many people to get them ready for the coming of the Light. Therefore, people called him John the Ready.
John: That's John the Baptist.

Narrator:	Oh, yeah. Well, John was a rather unusual fellow. He dressed mainly in camel's skin, *which went out of style several years ago.* If you think John smelled bad with the skin *on* him, you ought to smell the camel with the skin *off* him!
John:	Well, I may not make it with the outfit, but this belt is genuine leather!
Narrator:	Not only did John dress strangely—
John:	Not strangely . . . just different.
Narrator:	Not only did John dress, uh, different, but he also ate strangely, uh, differently.
John:	What's so bad about locusts with wild honey on them?
Narrator:	Yek!
John:	No taste for the finer things in life!
Narrator:	But no matter what John did, he had a message that people needed to hear.
John:	Repent, turn from your sins, the kingdom of heaven is closer than you think! You brood of vipers who—
Narrator:	You what? What does that mean?
John:	It means that they're all snakes in the grass!
Narrator:	Don't you think that's a little harsh?
John:	At this point it may be, but you didn't listen to the rest of the message!
Narrator:	All right, go on!
John:	Where was I? Oh, yes—you brood of vipers, who warned you to flee from the wrath to come? Start acting like you've asked for forgiveness and quit looking to the past for salvation!
Narrator:	Many people had questions: ordinary folk, tax collectors, and soldiers.
A Questioner:	What should we do?
John:	If you have two shirts, give one to someone who doesn't have any.
Tax Collector:	Sir, I was wondering what I should do?
John:	Don't collect any more than you should!
Soldier:	What about us?
John:	Don't take money by force, or accuse anyone falsely, and oh, don't go on strike for more money!
Narrator:	And as all preachers do, John kept on preaching.

John:	Now I am baptizing you with water, but there is one coming after me and he's greater than I am. I mean I can't even untie his shoelace without feeling unworthy! He's the one that will give you a different type of baptism. He's going to baptize you with the Holy Spirit!
Narrator:	Now while John was doing all of this, the priests of the Jews were doing something else.
Priest 1:	Doggone it, there is just no one attending our big temple bazaar because they're all out at John's revival meeting!
Priest 2:	I wish there was some way to get rid of John the Ready.
Narrator:	That's Baptist.
John:	Thank you.
Narrator:	You're welcome.
Priest 1:	Let's go talk to him. Maybe he's not as strange as we think.
Priest 2:	Did you ever eat locusts with honey on them?
Priest 1:	Yek!
Narrator:	The priests made their way out to where John was baptizing.
Priest 1:	I'll go ask him.
Priest 2:	All right.
Priest 1:	John, excuse me. But who are you?
John:	Whoever I am, I am not who you think I am!
Priest 1:	Well, I don't think you're anyone. I just wondered if you might think that you're someone special.
Narrator:	If John said he was the Messiah (the awaited deliverer), the priest would have him put to death for blasphemy (that is, claiming to be God).
Priest 2:	(as Priest 1 returns) Well, what did he say?
Priest 1:	He says he's no one special. So what do we do now?
Priest 2:	Did you ask him if he thought he was the Messiah?
Priest 1:	Well, I didn't say it right out.
Priest 2:	Why not?
Priest 1:	That camel skin smelled terrible, and I couldn't stand being too close to him! Y'know I got to thinking about that poor camel running around without his skin—naked as a blue jay—it sure must be cold!
Narrator:	Are you going to ask him or not?

Priest 1:	All right, all right! Are you the Messiah?
John:	No!
Priest 2:	Who are you then, Elijah?
John:	No!
Priest 1:	A prophet?
John:	No!
Priest 2:	Doggone, this is no fair. At least tell us animal, vegetable, or mineral.
John:	You're using up your Twenty Questions fast.
Priest 1:	Well, who are you? What do you say about yourself?
John:	I am a voice.
Priest 2:	I've never seen one of those before.
Priest 1:	What do you do?
John:	I cry in the wilderness!
Priest 1:	Why do you cry in the wilderness? Isn't it a lot nicer in your room, where Mom and Dad can help out?
Narrator:	Not boo-hoo cry. Preach-type cry. Like a town crier!
Priest 1:	Oh, what do you cry?
John:	Make straight the way of the Lord!
Priest 2:	Well, if you're not him why are you baptizing?
John:	I told you that there's one coming after me that is greater than I, and he's going to baptize with the Holy Spirit and with fire! As a matter of fact, he's standing right in this crowd somewhere! He is the Lamb of God who takes away the sins of the world!
Narrator:	The crowd began to get very quiet and a man moved out of the middle of the crowd and started walking toward John. The priests did not understand and left bewildered. As the man approached, something mysterious happened. All at once the clouds opened up and something that looked like a dove came down upon him. Many people had different reactions to this event. On that day this man made four followers. How would you react to this same man if he were to make the same sort of entrance today?

LANEY LOOKS AT THE CHRISTMAS STORY

Here's a skit for Christmas that can be performed with only three people: a lady (Mrs. Hansen), a little girl (Laney Joy), and a man's voice offstage for the father. The girl can be someone dressed like a little girl and acting like one. For best results, the lines should be memorized. The set can be a makeshift living room with a front door and perhaps a couch and some other simple furnishings.

Laney: (*singing*) Away in a manger, no crib for a bed,
The little Lord Jesus laid down his sweet head.
The stars in the sky looked down where he lay,
The little Lord Jesus, asleep on the hay.
The cattle are blowing, the baby awakes,
But little Lord Jesus, no crying he makes . . . (*Doorbell rings.*)

Father: Laney . . . Laney Joy! Will you get the door?

Laney: I would, Dad, but what if it's not a friendly person?

Father: It's probably Mrs. Hansen. Just tell her to wait downstairs until I'm finished with this appointment.

Laney: (*opens door*) Hello, lady.

Lady: (*very cheerfully*) Well, hello. You must be the preacher's little girl. I'm Mrs. Hansen. From church. I have an appointment with your dad. May I come in?

Laney: He's already got one 'pointment upstairs. I don't think he needs another one.

Lady: I don't think you understand, dear. You see—

Laney: In fact, I am certain that he does not need any. My mama always says that Papa has too many 'pointments.

Lady: (*mildly amused*) No, dear, you don't understand. I want to talk to your daddy about marrying my daughter.

Laney: Oh, lady, you're too late. My papa is already married. He married my mama a couple of years ago.

Lady: A *couple* of years?

Laney: Yes, lady. I think it was even before I was born, and I'm five years old.

Lady: Yes, I'm sure it was—

Father: Laney? Is that Mrs. Hansen?

Laney: Yes, Sir. I'm trying to tell her that you aren't innerested in marrying—

Father: Laney, just invite her in. I'll be with her in a few minutes.

Laney: Well, it's against my better judgment. But I guess I have to do what my papa says. Come in.

Laney: While we are waiting, I will entertain you.

Lady: Oh, that's not necessary, dear.

Laney: Oh, yes, lady. It's part of my role as the preacher's daughter. First I will tell you about myself. My name is Laney Joy, and I'm five years old, and I'm a very precarious child.

Lady: *(whispered)* I'm beginning to see that. *(aloud)* Precarious?

Laney: Yes. That means I'm ahead of other kids my same age. I can sing . . . and I can read the Bible all by myself.

Lady: Read the Bible? And you're only five?

Laney: Aren't you impressed, lady? Would you like to hear me read something?

Lady: Well, I, uh—

Laney: I know. Since it is nearly Christmas, I will read the Christmas story to you. Have you heard that one?

Lady: Yes, a few times.

Laney: But I bet you never heard it the way I read it.

Lady: Somehow I can believe that!

Laney: O.K. This is how it goes. Once upon a time, a long time ago, an angel came to Mary and said, "Mary, would you like to have the baby Jesus?" Mary said she guessed she would someday, after she married Joseph. But she did not know if she would name her first son Jesus. But the angel said that was not what he had in mind. He wanted to know if she would have the Son of God. Well, Mary did not know about that. She said she would have to think about it.

Lady: Wait. Are you sure that's the way the story goes?

Laney: Certainly. You don't think she would agree to something like that without thinking about it first, do you?

Lady: I guess I never thought about it quite that way.

Laney: You have to think about these things, lady. Anyway, Mary finally said she guessed it would be O.K., as long as she could wait until she married Joseph. Then they would want to wait until they had enough money to support a baby. But the angel said, "No way. Don't you ever read your Bible, Mary? 'Cause in the Bible it says that Jesus was born at just the right time. And that right time is right now.'' So Mary had to make up her mind quick. It was one of those now-or-never deals. You know about them, don't you, lady?

Lady: Well, yes. But not quite in that way. *(pauses)* So Mary decided to have the baby Jesus?

Laney: I was just coming to that next part. Mary said it would be O.K. with her if it was O.K. with Joseph. You can kinda see how he might not like it, can't you, lady?

Lady: I never thought about it before, but, yes, I can.

Laney: Well, the angel said if she was really worried about it, he would appear to Joseph in a dream and tell him all about it. But would she please make up her mind because he had to go on and do other things for God. So then Mary said O.K., she'd do it if the angel would promise her that everything would be all right. But you know what the angel said to that?

Lady: No, I don't.

Laney: The angel said he did not know what would happen. He only knew what God said to do. But he reckoned if Mary did what God wanted her to do, chances were things would turn out O.K. in the end. Then he quoted Hebrews 11:1 to her and left. So that's how it all began. Then you know what happened?

Lady: I used to think I did, but I'm not so sure now.

Laney: Well, next, Mary and Joseph had to go to Bethlehem to pay up their back taxes. You see, God had to get them to Bethlehem so what Micah had said would come true—about Jesus being born in Bethlehem—and God figured taxes were as good an excuse as any. My papa's been to the Holy Land—that's where Bethlehem is—and he says that's a hard trip even in a jeep. So you can imagine what it was like on a donkey. I bet by the time they got to Bethlehem Mary was sorry she ever got involved in the whole business. But that's not the kind of thing you can change your mind about, so she had to go through with it. But by the time they got to Jerusalem, I bet she was not singing that same song.

Lady: Song? What song was that?

Laney: 'Bout how her soul doth magnify the Lord. She was probably saying she'd just as soon somebody else had all that honor and let her just be a plain housewife—which was all she ever wanted anyway. You know, in one way it would have been nice if

God could have waited 'til today and let some women's lib lady have baby Jesus. But that was not God's style. He wanted Mary to do it. So they got to Bethlehem, but all the hotels were full 'cause Joseph hadn't phoned ahead for reservations. Then you know what happened?

Lady: They had to stay in a stable?

Laney: That's very good, lady. They had to stay in a stable 'cause there was not room for them in the Holiday Inn. Well, the angel was looking down at them, and you know what he did? He told God he did not think it was fair, making them have it so rough. And he offered to go down with a whole squad of other angels and sort of clean up the place, make it a little better looking since it would be the first place baby Jesus would see on earth. And if it was too bad it might make him change his mind and decide not to live on earth, after all. Well, God said that would be a shame, 'cause the world was counting on Jesus. But he would not let the angels come and fix things up. He said he'd already taken care of that.

Lady: Oh? How had he done that?

Laney: He made baby Jesus be just like any other human baby, so he wouldn't notice if he was born in a stable or a house or a palace. The angels said they guessed that was all right—they had not thought of it that way. Which is why God is God 'cause he had a better idea. Then the exciting part happened.

Lady: And what was that?

Laney: That was when the angels started singing "Glory to God in the Highest." The shepherds heard it, and they started singing "Do You Hear What I Hear?" Then the—

Lady: Now, wait a minute. I think you're confusing your stories.

Laney: I just elaborated a little, that's all. It *could* have happened. Anyway, the little drummer boy heard it, and he started playing his drum. And that was the first Christmas concert. All these people went to the stable and—oh lady, it was so exciting! *(Excitement builds, growing into awe.)* They saw baby Jesus, and they knew he was the Son of God, and they—lady, can you imagine what it was like? The Son of God on earth! So God would know what it was like to be a man 'cause that was the only way he could ever save people from their sins. Oh, lady, it must have been wonderful!

Lady: *(getting caught up in it, too)* Yes, it must have been!

Laney: I guess it was 'bout as wonderful as it is today.

Lady:	Huh? As *what* is today?
Laney:	As finding out that God came to earth.
Lady:	*(slightly puzzled)* Finding out that God came . . . ? *(understanding)* Oh, yes, I guess it *was* almost as exciting as that. And that's mighty exciting!
Laney:	Yes, lady. That's the truth! I cannot think of anything—
Father:	Good-by, Mr. Petersen. Hope I was able to help. *(louder)* Mrs. Hansen, I can see you now.
Lady:	Yes, pastor, I'll be right in. Laney Joy, thanks for the story.
Laney:	Oh, that's all right, lady. Any time. *(Laney resumes her song.)* Away in a manger, no crib for a bed . . . *(fade)*

LETTERS TO MAMA

For a unique understanding of the apostle Paul, have someone dressed as Paul's "Mama" read the following "letters" to the group. "Mama" should act and talk like a traditional Jewish lady about the time of Christ and introduce the letters before she reads them.

Dear Mama:

Peace from the God of our Fathers, from your distant son, Saul.

Well, Mama, I arrived safely. The ship sailed smoothly out to Cyprus, and we pulled in at Salamis around midday. I had plenty of time to visit Aunt Beulah.

By the way, little Elizabeth isn't little any more. She married the potter's son, a fine young man named Clypus. They're expecting their first by Purim. May all their children be boys! That reminds me, if I'm able to come home by spring I'll bring you some purple linen for sister Maria's wedding present. May she find a husband soon!

From there we traveled down the coast to Joppa. Then the long journey from the coast up to Jerusalem. By the time we saw the giant walls and magnificent gates, I was too tired to care. I headed straight for the Via Blanco. I recognized Mr. Benarma at once. He had received your letter and warmly welcomed me. His son Simeon will attend Gamaliel's classes with me.

After a day's rest, I took time to tour the city. What a thrill! Mama, you and Papa must come here some day. Imagine! I stood on the rock where Abraham stood. I saw with my own eyes the tomb of King David. I even touched with my own hands the giant stone blocks of Solomon's temple. Oh, may our eyes see the day when a lion from the Tribe of Judah reigns and rules in Jerusalem again. Perhaps next year by Passover.

The hatred for the Romans here is ten times worse than in Tarsus. And there are street-corner prophets all over the city. I even heard of a strange one out on the Jordan River. I must go out and see him, just for a laugh, of course. He seems to have the knack of making everyone mad at him. Just like the butcher there in Tarsus, right Mama?

Oh, and I must mention another one. He spends his time mainly up North, around Galilee. We hear rumors of his troublesome teachings. But don't worry about me. I won't have anything to do with such people. I'm here to learn of the God of our Fathers.

Please tell Papa the standard fees for Gamaliel's classes are more expensive than I thought. I will need to do some work for Mr. Benarma in the tent business to add a little income. If you happen to have an extra denarii or so, I know a poor, hard-working student who could put it to good use.

Give my love to Phineas, Elias, and Challa, also of course, to Maria and the rest of the family.

Greet one another with a holy kiss.

Your son, Saul

Dear Mama:

Peace from the Lord of Heaven, and from Saul, your obedient and faithful son.

I hope my long delay in writing to you caused no needless anxiety. I've been busy with studies of the Mikra and Talmud. Oh, Mama, the cloak you sent is beautiful. It fits just right and I wear it every cool day.

A few weeks ago we had some free time, so Simeon and Rabin and I walked out to the Jordan to hear the preacher I told you about. His name's John. What a sight! He wore an old camel skin and ranted like a mad man about King Herod. It didn't surprise me a bit to hear later that he had been arrested and thrown into prison.

Oh, yes, do you remember the one I mentioned from Galilee! Actually, he's a Nazarene—Jesus, by name. He's collected quite a following up North. He's a primitive moral teacher, at best. He has no academic background. Just a carpenter from Galilee. May the Lord of Heaven deliver us from these ignorant troublemakers!

I tell you, Mama, there's a great need for solid traditional teaching. Well, I suppose they'll arrest this one, too. So be it.

Tell Papa I certainly appreciate the ten denarii. Of course, it is all gone by now. But it did enable me to purchase half of the scrolls I needed. Now, if only I could buy the other half. . . .

I send this letter by Benjamin. Please tell me what's going on. He tells me nothing from Tarsus, only about Maria.

Greetings to all my friends.

Your wandering scholar son, Saul

Dear Mama:

Peace from your son, Saul.

Events here have been moving at a lightning pace. I'm preparing to take a trip to Damascus on official business of the high priest.

As you can tell, the handwriting is not my own. I'm dictating this letter to my secretary. Yes, I have some staff now. It comes with being Chairman of the Young Pharisees Council in Jerusalem. Most of my studies have been suspended because of the disturbances here. This Jesus of Nazareth—may his soul be in torment forever—kept stirring up the people in the North. We all knew it was just a matter of time until he made his move into Jerusalem.

He came during Passover. First, he convinced the people of Bethany—may God forgive their simple hearts—that he had raised one Lazarus from the dead. Yes, they really believed it. Then, he marched into the city leading an army of followers. He headed straight for the temple and threw all the merchants out.

Later, when I heard there was a reward for information leading to his arrest, I decided to investigate myself. But my effort was not needed. On the day before Sabbath, Simeon woke me.

"They got him," he said. "They arrested him last night."

We headed for the council. But to our amazement, the trial was over. I still don't know how they did it so quickly. Governor Pilate pronounced a capital-punishment verdict, and he was crucified with some other outlaws that same day.

The following week Rabin came up to me before class and said, "They claim the Nazarene is alive."

Can you believe it, Mama? People actually claim that a dead man lives again. Well, we all had a good laugh. However, several weeks later some of his followers showed up around town and disturbed the synagogue services with their wild tales. Not only did they say their master was alive, but they called him our longed-for Messiah.

At this point I couldn't restrain myself. The old Tarsus blood boiled. I had no idea the movement could be so blasphemous.

We arrested and imprisoned every follower we could find. We broke up every meeting, disrupted every teaching, and generally chased the whole lot out of Jerusalem.

But they only spread their lies into the countryside.

I made a personal appeal to the high priest (we're becoming quite good friends, Mama) and I received permission to travel throughout the area to arrest all I could find. You might say I'm the Chief Investigator.

Please, Mama, don't worry. They're not a violent lot. Usually they don't put up any resistance at all. I figure we'll have the whole mess cleaned up within the year. And it certainly won't hurt my status here in Jerusalem.

Don't expect me to write for a while. Tell Maria I'm so sorry to miss her wedding. May she be the mother of twelve sons! Benjamin is a good man. Treat him kindly, Mama.

Greet everyone in the love of the Holy One.

Your son, Saul

Dear Mama:

Grace and peace to you from God our Father and the Lord Jesus Christ.

Yes, Mama, you read right. The Lord Jesus Christ.

I know this must surely be the most difficult letter for you to understand. Please be patient and read through all I have to say.

I'm no longer enrolled at the school; I'm no longer living with the Benarmas; I'm no longer Chairman (or even a member) of the Young Pharisees Council. And, I'm no longer a restless, searching young man. I've found my peace before God our Father in heaven.

Where shall I begin?

I told you in my last letter I had an assignment in Damascus. It was almost noon on the last day of our trip when we could see the outline of the city on the horizon. Suddenly a bright light flashed around us.

Mama, you know I have always been truthful with you and Papa. You must believe what I say now. It was as if the very sun exploded before us. I was so frightened I fell to the ground on my face. All I could think was, "Surely this is the day of judgment, the coming day of our Lord!"

A voice boomed forth, "Saul, Saul, why are you persecuting me?"

I was petrified. I said nothing for a time, but then managed to ask hoarsely, "Who . . . who are you? Lord?"

"I am Jesus," the voice replied.

So, it was true after all. All my pious, self-righteous deeds filed before my eyes. I could see women and children crying as I dragged their husbands and fathers off to prison; I could see the poor body of Stephen as I screamed encouragement to those stoning him. By now the tears were streaming down my cheeks. I knew I was a dead man with nothing but Gehenna left to face.

"Oh, Lord," I cried. "What shall I do?"

This time the voice spoke not in condemnation, but rather in encouragement. "Rise up, stand on your feet. For this purpose I've appeared to you, to appoint you a minister and witness to me."

I was completely bewildered, so he said again, "Rise up and go into the city. There you will be told what to do."

When I stood up, I realized I was totally blind. I must have stumbled around, for my traveling companions grabbed me by the arm and escorted me into the city. All the time I kept thinking, what does this all mean? Is Jesus really the Messiah? Is he even more than the Messiah?

Three days later a stranger entered the house where I was staying. I felt his hands on my head and heard him say, "Brother Saul, the Lord Jesus who appeared to you on the road has sent me that you may regain your sight and be filled with the Holy Spirit."

Mama, how peaceful and powerful those words sounded. "Brother Saul," he called me, and immediately I could see again.

He then asked me, "Do you believe that this Jesus is the risen Christ?"

"Yes," I replied.

"Do you renounce the power of the world and the flesh and the Devil?"

I said yes, I did.

Oh, Mama, my heart is broken for you and Papa. How strange these words must seem to your eyes. All I can say is the truth and assure you of my love.

Greet one another with a kiss of love. And may the joy of the Lord Jesus soon dwell in each of your hearts.

Your faithful son, Saul

LX MINUTES

Here's a good skit for Easter, which is a takeoff on the television news program, *60 Minutes.*

Characters: Mikus Wallacius
        Caiaphas
        Petronius
        Galenius
        Mary Magdalene
        James

Wallacius: Good evening and welcome to LX Minutes. I am Mikus Wallacius and we are here at the tomb of Joseph of Arimathea on the outskirts of Jerusalem, Judea—the focal point of some very unusual happenings in the Roman Empire. This is where the body of Jesus of Nazareth was interred after his crucifixion. At the urging of the Jewish high priest and the Pharisees, the religious ruling class of the Jews, Pontius Pilate, the provincial governor, ordered his execution. This Jesus was a traveling rabbi and holy man. Because of his radical teachings and unorthodox methods (including reports of miracles and healings), he fell into disfavor with the strongly traditional, organized Jewish religious leaders. They had him arrested on the grounds of religious blasphemy and political insurrection, resulting in the death sentence rendered by Pontius Pilate. Three days after his execution the body disappeared from the tomb. The claim has been made that Jesus of Nazareth has risen from the dead, and rumors are rampant all over the city of his appearance to many individuals.

        The first person we will interview about this event that has rocked all of Palestine is Caiaphas, the high priest.

        Caiaphas, who *was* Jesus of Nazareth?

Caiaphas:	He was a blasphemer and a rabble-rouser. A mad carpenter from Nazareth who incited the people! He claimed to be the Messiah, the Son of God, and some of the people began to proclaim him king. He got what he deserved!
Wallacius:	Well, Caiaphas, now the corpse of Jesus is missing and your people seem to be very embarrassed by this. We have heard that Jesus claimed that after three days he would rise again from the dead. The rumor has spread all over Jerusalem that Jesus is alive and many people are convinced this is true. Do you believe Jesus came back to life as he said he would?
Caiaphas:	We pay *no* attention to his lunatic ramblings! I told you this blasphemer was insane!
Wallacius:	Well, Caiaphas, what happened to the body?
Caiaphas:	His disciples *stole* the body! They are responsible for perpetrating this hideous lie!
Wallacius:	This presents an extreme problem Caiaphas. Did you not request a guard from Pilate as well as place a detail of your temple guard at the tomb? You must have been aware of Jesus' claims?

Caiaphas:	Well, we, uh, . . .
Wallacius:	And did you not seal the entrance to the tomb with a 3000-lb. stone stamped in wax with the Imperial Seal of Rome?
Caiaphas:	Yes, but . . .
Wallacius:	How could, and why *would*, a ragtag group of eleven frightened men—men who all deserted Jesus in his greatest hour of need—overpower the Roman Legion, *your* temple guard, carry off a 2 1/2 ton stone, and make off with the body of a dead religious leader and leave behind the burial shroud and grave clothes!
Caiaphas:	You don't mean to tell me you believe this nonsense.
Wallacius:	We understand, Caiaphas, that you really had it in for Jesus because he pointed out the hypocrisy and corruption rampant in your religious system; for instance, the money changing scandal at the temple that made your father-in-law, Annas, a rich man. Allegations have been made that Jesus' trial was in gross violation of your Jewish law with false witnesses being brought against him and that since the disappearance of his body even members of your own sect, the Pharisees, are saying he was the Messiah—
Caiaphas:	I will discuss this nonsense and blasphemy *no longer! (stomps out)*
Wallacius:	Well? Our next interview is with Petronius Flavius, a centurion in the Roman Legion. Petronius, weren't you in command of the soldiers at the crucifixion of Jesus of Nazareth?
Petronius:	Yes, that is correct. My men also composed the guard at the tomb of Jesus.
Wallacius:	How many men were in the guard stationed at his tomb?
Petronius:	Sixteen men, fully armed with swords, shields, and spears, as well as some of the Jewish Temple Guard.
Wallacius:	The Pharisees have claimed that Jesus' followers stole his corpse to claim he arose from the dead. Could they have taken the body by force?
Petronius:	That would be impossible! The Roman Legionnaire is without equal as a fighting machine. Those sixteen men could have held that tomb against an army of one hundred men. And they would have—to the death.
Wallacius:	Is it possible that the guard fell asleep, and the disciples of Jesus were able to sneak in and make off with the body?

Petronius:	That is ridiculous! There's no way they could've removed the stone from the entrance of the tomb without waking half of Jerusalem. Besides that, the penalty for sleeping on your post is to be burned alive in front of the rest of the legion. The Jewish Sanhedrin cooked up that story and bribed their guards to keep quiet by promising to protect them from disciplinary action. They did this because they are so scared of this carpenter!
Wallacius:	You are the commander-of-the-guard. What did they report to you?
Petronius:	They were blinded by a great light and the earth shook. They were knocked to the ground, unconscious. When they came to, the stone was rolled away and the body was gone! They immediately came and woke me up and reported what had happened.
Wallacius:	This is incredible. Did you believe them?
Petronius:	These are seasoned, hardened soldiers who have served under me for years. They wouldn't lie to their commander.
Wallacius:	Well, Petronius, what do you think happened to the body in the tomb?
Petronius:	I have been a soldier for years and I have seen thousands die, but never did I see a man die like him. Truly, he was the Son of God. I'm convinced— he's alive.
Wallacius:	Thank you, Petronius. We now have Galenius, Governor Pilates' Press Secretary. Galenius, what is the official statement from the governor's office on the disappearance of the body of Jesus?
Galenius:	There is no official comment from Pilate. He has gone on a retreat to the coast of Lebanon for health reasons. The whole Jesus affair was distasteful to Pilate. He found no fault in the man, but the Jews demanded he be crucified. In compliance with their Passover tradition, he offered a pardon to a prisoner. They chose Barabbas, the revolutionary, and demanded the death of Jesus. He washed his hands of the whole ordeal when he handed Jesus over to be crucified.
Wallacius:	Well, Galenius, what do you think has happened?
Galenius:	I'm just as puzzled by this as anyone! How could a man rise from the dead? What happened to the body? If Jesus is alive and all those other stories I heard about him are true, then he must be some sort of god. I just wonder what sort of god would allow himself to be crucified?

Wallacius: Those are the questions we are trying to answer. Thank you for your time, Galenius. The next person we talked with was Mary Magdalene, a follower of Jesus and the first one to find that his body was missing. Mary, what happened that Sunday morning?

Mary Magdalene: At dawn that morning, some of the other women and I went to the tomb to finish anointing Jesus' body with spices. We were not able to finish the preparation for burial before the Sabbath and we went that morning to complete our task. Along the way we questioned ourselves as to who we would get to move the stone for us. When we arrived, we were shocked to see the stone already removed and when we discovered the body was gone, we were dismayed because we thought the authorities had taken the body of the Lord and hidden him from us. As we were weeping and confused, the angel of the Lord asked us why we were looking for the living among the dead, that Jesus was alive. This was more than we could handle and we could not take it in. I ran ahead of the older women to tell the disciples what had happened. None of them believed it—I wasn't sure I did either—and Peter and John ran all the way to the tomb leaving me behind. When they got there, they found the tomb empty—just as I had told them—and the grave clothes lying there like an empty cocoon. I had almost caught up with Peter and John when I saw a man, who I thought was the gardener, and I asked him if he knew where the Lord's body was. When he looked at me and called me by name, I then knew he was Jesus! My heart leapt within me! I went and told the disciples that I had seen the Lord! He appeared later that day to two of the disciples who were walking to Emmaus and later to all the disciples. He has appeared to us many times and explained what his death and resurrection, as foretold by the Scriptures, means. It is our salvation. He is the Messiah!

Wallacius: Mary, how did you become a follower of Jesus? Your background is not that of a religious person.

Mary Magdalene: No, it wasn't. Before I met Jesus I was a prostitute, and my life was controlled by demonic forces. All I wanted was to be loved, but I hated myself and I thought the only worth I had was to use my body as a sex object to try to find love.

Wallacius: How did Jesus change that?

Mary Magdalene: I always avoided the synagogues and felt condemnation from the religious leaders, but Jesus was different. He showed me the love of God and his forgiveness and delivered me from demonic possession and my life of sin. I am free and know I'm a child of God! You can have that same freedom! That's what Jesus' death and resurrection is all about!

Wallacius: Uh, thank you, Mary. Our next interview is with James, a member of the Pharisees and the brother of Jesus of Nazareth. James, were you a disciple of your brother Jesus?

James: NO! Jesus was always a source of tremendous embarrassment to me. I guess I resented him ever since we were little. I worked hard to study the Mosaic Law to become a Pharisee, but he was the one that never did anything wrong. And then when he began preaching to people! How would you feel if your brother was telling people he was the bread of life? I thought he was crazy. Here I was a Pharisee, a model citizen, and he was calling us a pit of vipers! Whitewashed tombs full of dead men's bones! That we were unclean and filthy on the inside! My embarrassment almost turned to hate. He violated the Sabbath, associated with riffraff and sinners and unclean people and then had the audacity to say our righteousness was filthy rags! I had tried to reason with him after that wedding at Cana but things got worse and worse as he did more and more outlandish things until finally I refused to acknowledge him as my brother.

Wallacius: Well, what happened when he was brought before the Sanhedrin and Pilate to be crucified?

James: I said nothing. He had claimed to fulfill prophecy and be the Messiah. That was blasphemy and warranted death. I wanted no one to know of my connection with him.

Wallacius: Did you go to his crucifixion?

James: No. I couldn't face that.

Wallacius: Well, what do you think of the reports that Jesus has risen from the dead?

James: They're not just reports. They are fact.

Wallacius: Are you sure? How do you know?

James: I have seen Jesus. I know he's alive!

Wallacius: Is this why you are now with Jesus' disciples?

James: Yes, it is! All of the Scriptures that never made sense to me have now come alive. Jesus was the fulfillment of the prophecies! He is the hope of Israel! The Messiah! He was not an embarrassment to me! I was an embarrassment to him in my hard-hearted self-righteousness and my foolish pride. It was necessary for him to suffer and die for all of our sins and then to rise again and conquer death. I am now willing to die for him who died for me. He is no longer my brother—he is my Lord and my God! You need to make him your Lord!

Wallacius: Well, thank you, James. *(to audience)* You have heard our interviews. What do you think? Is Jesus alive? If this man has risen from the grave as they say, what does that mean for us? Those who follow Jesus are willing to suffer persecution for his sake. They really believe he is alive. This Jesus has really affected a lot of people, even his detractors. *(visibly stirred)* I must investigate this further! Who was this carpenter from Nazareth? Did he rise from the dead? Let us hear your thoughts and comments. Write us at:

LX Minutes
CBS (Caesars Broadcasting System)
1800 Appian Way
Rome

A MAD LATE DATE

This skit is a good discussion-starter about family and parent-teen relationships.

Characters: Father
Mother
Daughter (Christy)
Son (Donald)

The setting is the breakfast table. Everyone except Christy is seated. Father is reading the paper, Mother is pouring coffee, and Donald is toying with his cereal. Christy hasn't come in yet.

Mother: Quit playing with your food, Donald. You'll be late for school.
Father: I'll have some more coffee, dear.
Donald: Speaking of being late, what about Christy last night? Man, if I came in that late, I'd be flogged till daylight.
Father: You let us worry about your sister. Anyway, you have to be able to get a date first.
Donald: Funny, funny!
Mother: You know, I am worried about Christy. This is the third time this has happened and— *(Christy enters and interrupts.)*
Christy: And every time there was a perfectly good excuse. Just like last night.
Donald: Some reasons! Out of gas, flat tires—what's it going to be this time?
Christy: It's none of your business, smart aleck.

Father:	Well, it is *my* business, Christy. You know how worried your mother and I become when you are late.
Mother:	Yes, you could have at least called and let us know you had problems.
Donald:	Kind of hard to find a phone booth out at Folsom Lake.
Christy:	Knock it off, bird brain. I couldn't call. Coming home from the game we stopped at Eppie's and the service was just terrible.
Mother:	Could you have called from there?
Christy:	No, Mom. We left in plenty of time—11:00. But we hit some traffic downtown because of the big fire. Just no way we knew that was going to happen.
Donald:	Ha! That greaser you were with probably planned the whole thing.
Father:	That's enough, Don. Christy, you know the rules around here. We've asked you to be in by 12:00 and this is the third time you've been late. I'm just going to have to ground you for one week.
Christy:	But Dad, you don't understand. We couldn't help it!
Father:	I know you have a good reason, but rules are rules. And this isn't the first time.
Christy:	So what if it's the fifteenth time? I couldn't help it and I don't think it's fair that I get grounded.
Donald:	Fair? It if had been me, I would have been chained and muzzled to the bed post for a month!
Christy:	Yeah, you *should* be chained and muzzled with that mouth of yours.
Mother:	Regardless, Christy, we must have some rules, and both of you have to obey them. I think your father is right. Anyway, I don't know if I like you dating that . . . that . . . oh, what is his name?
Donald:	You mean Greasy Gary?
Christy:	Shut up dummy! Now I know why I'm grounded. You never have liked anybody I've dated. If it wasn't him, you'd find something else—
Father:	*(Interrupts)* Now just a minute. The matter of liking who you're dating has nothing to do with it. I might say, however, you could be a little more choosey.
Christy:	Choosey! Who would you want me to date? One of those creeps at the church?
Mother:	Creeps? Where did you pick up that language?
Donald:	From Greasy Gary. I think that's his middle name.
Christy:	O.K., Smart-mouth—

Father:	Both of you calm down. If this is going to be your attitude, Christy, you can forget about going anywhere for the following week as well. Your mother and I could use a little help around here.
Christy:	What? You can't be serious! What about Donald? All he does is sit around and flap his mouth making corny jokes.
Mother:	Now, Christy, that's enough. There's no need to bring your brother into this. I think it is time we be just a little more considerate of each other.
Christy:	Why don't you start with me? I come in a lousy forty-five minutes late, and you act like it were three hours. Then you start harping on whom I date. All you're concerned about is your silly rules and regulations.
Father:	You don't need to raise your voice to your mother. And rules and regulations are something to be concerned about. But more important is your behavior within those rules. Either you shape up or else.
Donald:	Or shape out . . . that shouldn't be hard for you.
Christy:	(in tears) I've had enough! I'm leaving! Nobody understands me. You just don't care.
Mother:	We do care Christy. You are the one who doesn't understand. Why, when I was your age—
Christy:	Now comes the second lecture! Well, times are different, and you are *not my age!*
Father:	I think I've heard enough. Both of you get off to school, and Christy, I want you home at 4:00 sharp.

MARY'S STORY

Excellent during the holiday season, this skit is based on the Christmas story. However, it is perhaps even more effective when presented at a time other than Christmas to heighten the element of surprise at the ending. The names of the characters are not revealed during the play itself; the setting is modern times. Each of the scenes can be set up any way you choose, and the dialogue has been written in such a way as to allow you the freedom to change or add to it as you see fit.

Characters: Mary
               Joseph
               Mom
               Dad
               Girl 1 and 2 (Mary's Friends)
               Carpenters 1 and 2
               Teachers 1 and 2
               Neighbors 1 and 2
               Elizabeth
               The Doctor
               The Psychiatrist
               The Rabbi

Scene One (girls sitting around a table discussing the upcoming dance)

Girl 1:   What are you going to wear?
Mary: I don't know if I'm going.
Girl 2:   Everybody's going. It'll be a good dance.
Mary: I can't even dance. Anyway, I wouldn't know how to ask a guy for a date.
Girl 1:   This is your chance to get around.
Girl 2:   What about that guy your parents like? Do they still want you to marry him when you get out of school?
Girl 1:   I hear he's got his own business and a sharp car.
Girl 2:   The guy I'm going with has a new Corvette.

Scene Two (Mary kneeling beside her bed)

Mary: (This can be ad-libbed somewhat.) Why me? What am I going to tell Mom and Dad? What will my friends think? What is he going to do? They're never going to believe me.

Scene Three (Mary's parents sitting on the couch in the living room)

Mom: Well, I asked her what was wrong, but I wasn't able to get much out of her. She claims there's a lot of pressure from her teacher giving her a big assignment.

Dad: Well, that doesn't sound like our little girl. She doesn't usually let something like that bother her so much. I've heard a lot about the drug problem at her school. I'm sure our daughter has been raised well enough not to do anything like that, but that doesn't mean the pressure isn't hurting her. Maybe I could talk to her.

Mom: Well, I guess it couldn't hurt but be careful not to hurt her more. She's been awfully touchy lately.

Scene Four (*two girls talking on the phone*)

Girl 1: I'm worried about her. She's been acting strange lately, crying about silly things.

Girl 2: Yeah, I've noticed.

Girl 1: Have you noticed she's gained weight?

Girl 2: Yeah, maybe it's from all that broccoli and other health food she's been eating.

Girl 1: She won't go out with us, not even to the dance we all went to. She says she's too tired.

Girl 2: She's had the flu a lot lately. Maybe I'll call her and see how she's feeling.

Scene Five (*the teacher's lounge at school*)

Teacher 1: She's been acting differently lately.

Teacher 2: Her grades sure have dropped, and she's been missing my class a lot.

Teacher 1: She seems lonely. She isn't around her old crowd anymore.

Teacher 2: She's also been putting on weight and wearing those loose tops.

Teacher 1: She's in my first-hour English class, and she's asked to see the nurse a lot. Do you think she's in trouble? She's so sweet.

Scene Six (*two neighbors talking over the back fence*)

Neighbor 1: I just *know* she is! And with those wonderful parents, too. They've tried so hard to bring her up right.

Neighbor 2: I bet I know who the father is—that older boy her father knows. He's the only one I've seen at the house.

Neighbor 1: You never know, do you? She just didn't seem the type. She's so well behaved and respectful.

Neighbor 2: She goes to Synagogue every week. What is the world coming to?

Scene Seven (two carpenters sawing boards)

Carpenter 1: Poor guy, that's too bad.
Carpenter 2: He's got to be crazy to marry her.
Carpenter 1: I'd hate to be in his place.
Carpenter 2: Be quiet, he's coming.

Scene Eight (In the living room Mom and Dad are talking to Mary and Joseph when three men enter.)

Mom: Where did I go wrong? *(Doorbell rings. Dad gets up to answer it and escorts in three men.)*

Dad: Gentlemen, we have discovered our daughter is pregnant and we don't know what to do. We need your expert opinions about what we should do. We don't want her life and future ruined.

Doctor: As a physician, the only option I can see for a girl her age is to terminate the pregnancy. If you choose abortion, we'll have to act quickly. Then no one else will have to know.

Psychiatrist: From the viewpoint of a psychiatrist, her emotional stability would probably stand an abortion better than adoption. If you choose for her to give birth to the child, she might want to keep it, and I believe that would be a grave mistake.

Rabbi: They must get married. I know they're young, but with prayer the marriage can work.

Dad: *(To Joseph)* You got her into this—what do you have to say?

Mary: I'm going to have my baby and keep him. With the Lord's help, I can handle it.

Joseph: I had considered breaking it off, but I've prayed about the situation and have decided it's God's will that we should be married. I'll do my best to be a good father to the baby.

Scene Nine (the living room with Mary and Elizabeth)

Mary: He wonders whether or not our marriage will work. I want it to work.
Elizabeth: He's a quiet person who loves his work. I'm sure he's worried about the gossip you've told me about.

Mary:	Yes, I feel its affecting our relationship. He's so practical that he can't believe how I got pregnant. No one believes him when he says he isn't the father.
Elizabeth:	I understand what you are going through, but we know it will be worth it. When the baby is born, everything will be O.K., you'll see.
Mary:	You're only my cousin, but you're more like a sister to me.

Scene Ten (Mary and Joseph)

Mary:	I'm really frightened about your leaving on this trip. The doctor says that the baby could come anytime now.
Joseph:	Yeah, I know but I have to go! The only solution is having you go with me.
Mary:	Well, I'd rather be with you when the time comes. You know, I am really excited about the baby. God has given me peace that we have done the right thing.
Joseph:	I really feel that way, now. We have a big job ahead of us. We first of all must be sure that we are completely dedicated to God so we can guide our little son.

Scene Eleven (Mary and Joseph with the new baby. The doctor, the psychiatrist, and the rabbi enter, bringing gifts for the baby. They kneel and worship him.)

Doctor:	(to Mary and Joseph) Forgive us, for our prejudice and judgments. We are here to give you and your son our love.
Psychiatrist:	Through prayer we were able to understand your situation.
Rabbi:	Mary, what will you name him?
Mary:	He has been named . . . Jesus.

MELODY IN F

Here's a great way to tell the story of the Prodigal Son. Have someone memorize this script for best results.

Feeling Foot-loose and Frisky, a Feather-brained Fellow
Forced his Fond Father to Fork over the Farthings,
And Flew Far to Foreign Fields
And Frittered his Fortune Feasting Fabulously with Faithless Friends.

Fleeced by his Fellows in Folly, and Facing Famine,
He Found himself A Feed Flinger in a Filthy Farmyard.
Fairly Famishing, He Fain would've Filled his Frame
With Foraged Food from Fodder Fragments.
"Fooey, my Father's Flunkies Fare Far Finer,"
The Frazzled Fugitive Forlornly Fumbled, Frankly Facing Facts.
Frustrated by Failure, and Filled with Foreboding,
He Fled Forthwith to his Family.
Falling at his Father's Feet, he Forlornly Fumbled,
"Father, I've Flunked,
And Fruitlessly Forfeited Family Favor."

The Far-sighted Father, Forestalling Further Flinching,
Frantically Flagged the Flunkies to
Fetch a Fatling from the Flock and Fix a Feast.

The Fugitive's Fault-Finding brother Frowned on
Fickle Forgiveness of Former Folderol.
But the Faithful Father Figured,
"Filial Fidelity is Fine, but the Fugitive is Found!
What Forbids Fervent Festivity?
Let Flags be un-Furled! Let Fanfares Flare!"

Father's Forgiveness Formed the Foundation
For the Former Fugitive's Future Fortitude.

MELODY IN S

Here's the story of the Good Samaritan in the key of S.

Sure enough, the Scholarly Scribe Stood up and Slyly Said to the Savior, "Sir, Surely you Surmise that I Seek a Sustained Subscription to a Solid life beyond the Solid Shale Sepulcher. So what Steps Shall I Secure for Such a Subsistence?

The Savior Said, "What Saith the Statutes?" The Stupid Scribe responded, "It Says, 'Serve,

Sigh for, and Sway with your Savior with all your Substance, Soul, Spirit, and Strength. And Sway with the Sire who Settles by your Side as you Sway with yourself.' "

"Sure," said the Savior, "Stay So and you Shall Survive." So, the Silly Scribe, Seeking to Save his Skin, Said, "Sir, I Solicit you to Set before me my Sidekick." The Savior Sent home his Statement by citing a Sample:

A Sorry Sap was Sauntering Slowly Side-to-Side when Suddenly Six Serious assassins Set themselves to Smash that Silly Sap. Stripped, Stunned, and Shaken, he Stumbled and Sank to the Solid Slate of the Sidewalk. After Seemingly Several Seconds Slipped by, a Slothful Sort of celibate Saw the Simple Soul Seething on the Sidewalk. So, he Stopped and then Simply Strolled by. Soon a Selfish Shepherd who Subsisted on a Small Salary Stalled a Second and left the Sorry Simpleton Stranded. Suddenly, a Stalwart Samaritan Slid Straightway to the Subdued Subject who was Stunned. Seeing the Seriousness of the Situation, he restored the Strength of that Sorry Soul and Sitting him in the Saddle of his Staunch Stallion, Surveyed him Safely to Some Septic Sanatarium, where he Secured Some Serious Substantial Sleep for that Stranded Sojourner.

"So," Said the Savior, "Seeing such circumstances, who Seems to be the Sympathetic Saint in Such a Situation?"

"Surely, the Samaritan," Stammered the Scribe.

"Superb," Said the Savior, "So must you Shape yourself."

MICROCOSM

As a good dramatization to emphasize the need for world missions, this program can be presented to the entire congregation with effective results.

The setting: At a small table on the platform, four speakers sit with microphones. They carry on a conversation similar to the one below. (You should adapt it to present an accurate picture of your own church's mission program.)

SCRIPT:

1: You all have a copy of next year's budget and projections. What do you think?

2: This is the same as last year's! All of our costs have gone up! And we need to send out more people! How can we keep the same figures as last year?

3: He's right. Transportation, printing, equipment—all are way up from last year. And food costs have skyrocketed in the Philippines and Irian Jaya because of the droughts. How can we expect our missionaries to get by on this? Let alone expand their ministries!

1: You all know that we've had trouble making our budget these last few years. If the money doesn't come in, we can't spend it. It's been a step of faith even to come up with this budget, yet we're confident that God will supply. But it will mean sacrifice.

4: The people in our churches give to missions and God has blessed our work so far. But some still don't see missions as being very important.

2: Don't they see the need? Don't they understand the number of lost souls out there?

4: Well, probably not. We try our best to educate the churches, but remember most of them haven't had the kind of exposure to overseas missions we have. Most don't realize how many are lost.

1: On top of that, some are hesitant to give to missions because they don't think they can afford it.

4: Or else they feel that we have enough missionaries now.

3: Enough missionaries! (pause) Enough missionaries. Jesus said, "The harvest is plentiful but the workers are few." That's still true today.

2: In Bogota we have eight missionary families in a city of almost three million! We have only two in Bombay, and eighteen in the entire country of Upper Volta! Even with the national pastors and evangelists, it's a huge task. There are so many people . . .

3: And so many forces working against us. There are all the false religions. And the cults work overseas, too.

1: God has called us to a difficult task. There's no doubt about that. But he's also promised to equip us for that task. Nothing is impossible when we're in God's will.

3: That's right.

2: I wish people would stop seeing missions as an extra or as something for somebody else to do. Jesus told us to go. If we can't go ourselves, we can at least support those who go.

4: Well, Jesus also told us to pray that God would send laborers into his harvest. Let's pray that the Holy Spirit will work in the churches. He can convince people of the needs much better than we can. If he does, and people listen, we will be able to expand the work.

During this dialogue, other young people are circulating quietly throughout the congregation trying to get converts. They distribute literature for their religion, asking people if they would like to "follow Buddha" or "worship the Spirit of the River," and so on. These young people may wear appropriate costumes, although it's not really necessary, and play the following roles:

1 Christian
2 Hindus
3 Moslems
1 Confucian
1 Buddhist
1 Communist (or atheist)
2 Worship the Spirit of the River
2 Worship the Sun
2 Worship the Spirits of their Ancestors

(When the speakers on the platform have finished, the "missionaries" who have been circulating in the congregation come to the front and introduce themselves.)

Ancestor, Sun, and River Worshipers: We are animists. We worship many different spirits in nature.

Communist: I am a Communist. I do not believe in any God.

Buddhist: I follow the teachings of Confucius.

Moslems: We are Moslems. Our god is Allah.

Hindus: We are Hindus. We worship many gods.

Christian: I am a Christian. I follow Jesus Christ. God does not want anyone to perish, but many in the world are lost because they do not know Jesus. Please, help me to tell them.

After the skit, explain to the congregation that the people in the line are proportioned by religion in approximately the ratio as the world population. Christians are outnumbered fourteen to one.

THE NIGHT BEFORE EASTER

Here's a short skit developed as an opening for Easter morning Sunday school. It depicts a conversation between Peter and John in an upper room where they're hiding the night before the Resurrection. The dialogue focuses on Peter's grief over having denied Jesus, and how he can't possibly make it right with the Lord now that he's gone.

   The skit should be memorized for the best effect. It can be followed up with a Bible study on forgiveness and on how Jesus is willing and able to forgive us when we feel we have let him down (focus especially on John 21:15–19).

Setting: Peter and John are lying on the floor sleeping.
Peter: *(suddenly beginning to toss and turn, mumbling)* I'm sorry, Master, I'm sorry! *(The more he tosses and turns, the louder the words get until he finally sits up straight,*

	murmuring *loudly, almost frantically.)* I'm sorry, master! I'm sorry! *(burying his face in his hands and whimpering)* I'm sorry, so sorry.
John:	*(John is awakened by the noise. He reaches over and touches Peter's arm.)* What is it Peter? What's wrong?
Peter:	I had a terrible nightmare. I'm sorry if I woke you.
John:	*(with a short, quiet laugh)* I'm afraid it wasn't much of a sleep to be awakened from. I'm tired, but sleep isn't coming very easily to me tonight.
Peter:	My sleep is fitful enough without the nightmares.
John:	What are these nightmares you're having?
Peter:	Actually, it's the same one over and over again. I'm standing in the courtyard of the high priest's house. As I look in the window, I can see the Master looking at me. He has the saddest look on his face I've ever seen. I know that I've denied him, but when I try to apologize, he turns his head away from me! *(in a broken voice)* I denied him, John! I swore that I didn't know him when I promised that I would stand by him no matter what!
John:	I think I understand what you're feeling, Peter.
Peter:	*(bewildered)* How can *you* understand what I'm feeling? You stood by him faithfully right up to the end. You stood at the cross with his mother. He spoke with you! How did you deny him?
John:	Isn't my hiding here in this room with you a form of denial, too? I may not have betrayed him with words, but my actions speak loudly enough.
Peter:	*(more relaxed)* Forgive me, John, I know this has been hard on all of us. It just seems that I was always giving the Master some kind of trouble. Remember when I tried to keep him from coming to Jerusalem in the first place? He called me Satan! And when I lashed out with my sword in the garden, he rebuked me. I swore that I would lay down my life for him if necessary, but when the time came, I denied him and ran. I've failed him time and time again, John, and now he's dead and I can't make it right!
John:	I'm sure we all wish we had done differently. How do you think *I'm* feeling? He put me in charge of his mother! How can I take care of her when the soldiers are sure to be looking for us next?
Peter:	The present doesn't concern me, John, it's the future that I'm thinking about. Remember what the Master said to us? He said that if anyone denied him before

men, he would deny them before the Father. How can I go on through life with the burden of guilt that's mine because I betrayed him? I wanted to speak up for him, but I feared for my life. Now that fear may cost me eternity!

John: *(Both men sit quietly for a few moments. Then John speaks up.)* These past few days have left me confused. He was always telling us that he was going to die, but I never thought it would be so soon. What do you think will become of us now that he's gone?

Peter: He told us himself that we could expect the same treatment they would give to him. I fear that we may soon join him!

John: Maybe he'll rise from the dead as he promised! We saw him raise Lazarus, but could he possibly raise himself?

Peter: I hope that for *your* sake he does, John. But even if he did come back, I fear that our friendship would never be the same because of what I've done.

John: He was a man of forgiveness and understanding, Peter. I'm sure he would forgive you. *(Both men fall silent again.)*

John: *(John stares off into space for a moment as if thinking. Suddenly a smile comes across his face.)* It sure was a wonderful three years, wasn't it, Peter? All that he said and did is so vivid in my mind—I'll never forget it. I remember best how much he loved us, how I could feel that love so strongly, even when he wasn't there. *(looking sadly at the floor)* I loved him so much. Never have I had a better friend.

Peter: Yes, he was a remarkable man, and a good friend and teacher. Well, we really should try to get some sleep. Only God knows what tomorrow holds for each of us.

John: *(Both men lie back down on the floor, but neither closes his eyes. They are silent for a few moments, then John speaks up.)* Peter, you once said he was the Messiah. Do you still believe that?

Peter: Yes, I do. But will believing it bring him back? *(fade out)*

NOT GUILTY?

This one-act play takes place in a courtroom. It is based on the question, "If you were put on trial for being a Christian, would there be enough evidence to convict you?" This drama will be much more effective if the actors have memorized and rehearsed their lines enough to be comfortable with them.

The cast:	The Narrator
	The Prosecutor
	The Defense Lawyer
	The Judge
	Mr. Jones (store owner)
	Miss Roxie Smith (teenager)
	Mrs. Farkenparker (older lady)
	Sally
	Mike
	Bailiff
Props:	Desk and chair
	Judge's gavel
	Judge's robe
	Shawl and ladies hat (Mrs. F.)
	Letterman's jacket (Roxie)
	2 tables and chairs (defense and prosecuter's tables)
Scene:	Empty Courtroom (lights come on)

Narrator: What you are about to see could very well be a glimpse into the near future. The setting is a courtroom somewhere in America and the defendants are two young people accused of a rather unusual crime—Christianity.

Jesus said in Matthew 7 that you can tell a Christian simply by examining the fruit of his life. The court will soon be doing some "fruit inspection" of these young people's lives—will there be enough evidence to convict either of them of being a Christian? The court proceedings will be beginning very soon so sit back and relax. After all, you're not on trial for your faith, at least not yet.

Prosecutor: (Defense attorney, prosecutor, and witnesses all enter. Witnesses are seated. Defense attorney and prosecutor meet at the defense table and are casually chatting.) So! We meet again in the arena called the courtroom.

Lawyer: So we do.

Prosecutor:	I do so enjoy our little confrontations here, even though I do seem to put most of *your* clients behind bars for a multitude of crimes. Oh, don't get me wrong, I know you do as well as you possibly can defending the slime of society.
Lawyer:	Slime of society? My clients are all innocent until proven guilty!
Prosecutor:	Yeah, innocent like the burglar who was caught coming out of the art museum carrying several priceless paintings. When asked about them, he said that he had painted them himself! C'mon, you think he was innocent?
Lawyer:	You and I both know that the guy was framed!
Prosecutor:	O.K., how about those guys who robbed the bank and, with money in hand, ran out and jumped into the back seat of a squad car and yelled, "Get moving cabbie before the cops get here!"? You think they were innocent?
Lawyer:	Entrapment is what I call it! We're going to appeal that one.
Prosecutor:	Innocent until proven guilty, HA! I'm going to bury your two "innocent" clients today and you know it! By the time I get done with them, the judge won't be able to come up with anything else but "Guilty of Christianity!" Your clients don't have a prayer! Pardon my pun.
Lawyer:	We'll see!
Prosecutor:	Yes, we *will* see.
Bailiff:	(*Prosecutor turns and goes over to the prosecutor's table. The bailiff escorts the two defendants into the courtroom. They are seated at the defense table and begin to confer with their lawyer. The bailiff stands beside the judge's table. The judge opens the door)* All rise. *(He waits for judge to be seated then continues.)* This court is now in session. *(Everyone sits down except the bailiff.)*
Judge:	Let me see now. *(shuffles through papers)* Yes, here it is. *(looks at paper and then at the two defendants)* It seems that today we will be trying you two for a crime against society called Christianity. Prosecuting attorney, would you like to make your opening statement for the court, please?
Prosecutor:	*(Prosecutor stands and paces around while speaking.)* I'd be happy to, Your Honor. In this courtroom today I shall prove without a shadow of a doubt that these two *(points at defendants)* are guilty of a crime that

subverts the people of our society. It is a crime that causes people to start thinking of others first, a crime that makes people give freely of their finances to churches. The crime these two shall be proven guilty of is a crime that changes the entire thought process and lifestyle of those practicing it. The crime—Christianity!

Yes, I know, it sends shivers up and down my spine just to think that these two young people could be so easily involved at such an early age. It used to be, according to many, a crime of adults who were tired of society's ways. The youth were exempt since they had too many things going on in their lives to think seriously about becoming a Christian. Now even the youth of our society are affected by this crime of Christianity as we can see plainly here today. I shall seek, therefore, to make public examples of these two today! *(Prosecutor returns to the table and is seated.)*

Judge:	Would the defense like to make their statement?
Lawyer:	Indeed we would, Your Honor. *(Lawyer rises and paces around while speaking.)* Your Honor, through the process of this trial today, I shall prove without any doubt that my two clients *(points to defendants)* are not guilty of anything even resembling Christianity. I shall prove that, even though they were brought up in the church, they have not, nor ever will be, affected by such teachings of Christianity.

Your Honor, please look at my clients. Would nice looking, outgoing young people such as these ever get involved in such teachings as the prosecution proposes? I say no! They're young, they're vivacious. They have parties and school activities and even MTV available to them—why would they want to become Christians?

No, these are not criminals. They are but two young people caught in a vicious trap of gossip. There is no truth to the claims that they are Christians and I shall have *no* problem proving that! *(Lawyer returns to his seat.)*

Judge:	All right, now that we've heard both of your statements, let the trial begin. Bailiff, call in the first witness please.

Bailiff:	The court calls Mr. Jones to the witness stand. *(Mr. Jones goes directly to the witness stand and stands facing the bailiff.)*
Bailiff:	Raise your right hand. Do you promise to tell the truth, the whole truth, and nothing but the truth?
Mr. Jones:	I do.
Bailiff:	You may be seated.
Prosecutor:	*(rises)* Mr. Jones, please state your relationship to the accused.
Mr. Jones:	Well, I own a hardware store. It's called Jones Hardware Store, kind of a unique name for a store, don't you think?
Prosecutor:	Please, Mr. Jones, your relationship to the accused?
Mr. Jones:	Oh, well, Mike and Sally both work for me at my store. They've been with me for a couple of years now.
Prosecutor:	So, they work for you do they?
Mr. Jones:	Yes.
Prosecutor:	Then would you say that you know them rather well?
Mr. Jones:	I think so.
Prosecutor:	O.K., let's talk about Sally first. Has she ever given you any reason to think that she was a Christian?
Lawyer:	Objection, Your Honor! The prosecution is asking for an opinion.
Judge:	Sustained.
Prosecutor:	Let me put it this way, Mr. Jones, has she ever acted differently than any of your other employees?
Mr. Jones:	Well . . .
Prosecutor:	Yes, Mr. Jones?
Mr. Jones:	Well, there was this time when we ran a sale on some dust busters at our store.
Prosecutor:	Go on.
Mr. Jones:	O.K., we were running this special price on the new dust buster. We called it our "special price on new dust buster sale"—kinda catchy, don't you think.
Prosecutor:	Mr. Jones, please.
Mr. Jones:	O.K., O.K. We were running our sale and it was going so good we sold out all our dust busters. All we had left was the one that we use in the back-

	room shop. Boy, we use that thing for just about everything! It picks up dirt, dust, lint, sawdust, paper. . . .
Prosecutor:	Mr. Jones! What does that have to do with Sally.
Mr. Jones:	Well, that being the last one and all, I put it in a new box and sealed it up. Then I told Sally to sell it as new to old Mrs. McGillicutty who was wanting one.
Prosecutor:	And?
Mr. Jones:	She wouldn't do it. She said it was wrong and that it would be lying to tell her it was new.
Prosecutor:	Lying, eh? Go on.
Mr. Jones:	She said she couldn't because . . .
Prosecutor:	Because what, Mr. Jones?
Mr. Jones:	Because . . . she was a Christian.
Prosecutor:	A Christian! She *said* she was a Christian!
Lawyer:	I object!
Judge:	Overruled.
Prosecutor:	So, Mr. Jones, she claimed to be a Christian. Well, how about Mike? *(points at defendant)* He ever done anything like that or claimed that he was a Christian to you?
Mr. Jones:	No, Mike's a good boy but he never has given me reason to think that— *(interrupted by prosecution)*
Prosecutor:	No further questions, Your Honor. *(sits down)*
Judge:	*(looks to defense lawyer)* Your witness.
Lawyer:	*(stands and approaches witness)* Mr. Jones, would you care to finish your last statement please? "Mike never has given me any reason to think" what?
Mr. Jones:	Mike never has given me any reason to think that he is a Christian is what I was going to say.
Lawyer:	Assuming that you had asked Mike to sell the dust buster, do you think he would have?
Prosecutor:	Objection!
Judge:	Overruled. Mr. Jones, please answer the question.
Mr. Jones:	No doubt in my mind, yes! It was his idea in the first place.

Lawyer:	Mike's idea to lie and deceive old Mrs. McGillicutty?
Mr. Jones:	Yes.
Lawyer:	Now back to your account of Sally's alleged confession that she was a Christian. Isn't it true that you are a little hard of hearing and that what you *heard* her say was not that she was a Christian, but rather that she was a Norwegian and it goes against her morals to lie? Isn't this what actually happened—you can't hear very well so you heard something entirely different? Well, Mr. Jones?
Mr. Jones:	No way! I can hear real well with my hearing aid in.
Lawyer:	Let's test your hearing, Mr. Jones. *(pause)* What is the circumference of a marble?
Mr. Jones:	What?
Lawyer:	*(turns and walks away)* I rest my case, the man's stone-deaf! No further questions.
Judge:	You may step down, Mr. Jones.
Mr. Jones:	*(turns to judge)* What is the circumference of a marble?
Judge:	Please step down. Next witness please. *(Mr. Jones goes back to seat.)*
Bailiff:	The court calls Miss Roxie Smith. *(Miss Smith stands before the witness chair and faces the bailiff.)*
Bailiff:	Raise your right hand. Do you promise to tell the truth, the whole truth, and nothing but the truth?
Miss Smith:	You bet!
Judge:	A simple yes would suffice, Miss Smith.
Miss Smith:	O.K., yes, I do.
Bailiff:	You may be seated.
Prosecutor:	*(stands and approaches witness)* So, Miss Smith—
Miss Smith:	Oh, you can call me Roxie. It's short for Roxanne but everybody calls me Roxie so you can too.
Prosecutor:	All right. So Roxie, how do you know the two defendants?
Miss Smith:	Well, it's kinda like they sorta go to my school and, like, their lockers are sorta kinda like next to mine, you know, and—
Prosecutor:	*(interrupts)* So you attend school together, right?
Miss Smith:	Well, like, that was what I was saying, I think.

Prosecutor:	Roxie, first let me ask you about Sally. Is Sally any different than any of the other kids at school?
Miss Smith:	Of course she is! Can you imagine us all being exactly the same? Like gag me! If I was like Sue Ellen Pudski, I would just die—those ugly clothes and greasy hair!
Prosecutor:	No! No! No! It's taken for granted that everyone looks different. What I mean is, does she act any differently or talk any differently than the rest of the kids at school? Would she be considered, shall we say, peculiar?
Miss Sn_.h:	Oh, I know what you mean now. Why sure she acts different, she's a Christian.
Lawyer:	Objection, Your Honor! The prosecutor is leading the witness.
Judge:	Overruled.
Prosecutor:	You say she's a Christian, eh? Why do you say she is a Christian?
Miss Smith:	Well, I noticed she was always real nice to everybody and she was always happy. She never talked dirty and she never cut anyone down. I wondered what she had that made her this way so I up and asked her. I said, "Sally, what's different about you anyway? I can't figure you out." She told me she was that way because of the fact that she was a Christian and it was God's love coming out through her.
Prosecutor:	She told you she was a Christian?
Miss Smith:	Yeah, she not only told me that but she also told me how I could become one, too.
Prosecutor:	Unbelievable! Not only does the defendant break the law, she encourages others to as well! Do you know if she ever talked of this Christianity to anyone else at school?
Miss Smith:	Oh, all the time and to anyone who would listen. She even did a speech on it in our speech class.
Prosecutor:	Sounds to me like there was no remorse felt by her for being a Christian. *(points to Sally)* She is a hardened criminal, wouldn't you say, Roxie.
Miss Smith:	If that's a crime to believe in God and tell others about him, then . . . I guess so.
Prosecutor:	Now Roxie, tell me about the criminal's brother Mike. I suppose he's even worse—more bold, more willing to, so to speak, "Preach the gospel" to his friends.

Miss Smith:	Well . . . no, I don't think so.
Prosecutor:	What do you mean? Surely he is involved in this crime, too. Tell us about how he speaks to everyone about God, tell us how active he is in propagating the Christian message, tell us the hair-raising story of how he converts others to this unlawful belief!
Miss Smith:	I'd like to tell you but I just can't.
Prosecutor:	Why? Because you love him and are pledged to secrecy?
Miss Smith:	No, there's just nothing to tell. The only thing I know of is that he goes to a place called "church" with Sally every week.
Prosecutor:	Aha! So he is a Christian! *(to defense)* Your witness. *(Prosecutor is seated. Defense lawyer approaches the witness.)*
Lawyer:	Miss Smith—
Miss Smith:	Call me Roxie, it's short for—
Lawyer:	O.K., O.K.! Roxie, you say you've seen Mike go to a place called "church" right?
Miss Smith:	Well, no, I've never seen him go.
Lawyer:	So, how do you know he goes? Did he tell you?
Miss Smith:	Well, no, but I heard that he does.
Lawyer:	You heard that he goes? *(to judge)* She *heard* that he goes to church—does that sound like facts admissible in court? No! Miss Smith I propose that you hear many things that are not true. I propose that not only did you make up the story about Mike but that you also made up the story about Sally, too! I don't think she ever talked to you. I don't think she ever mentioned the word "Christianity" to you. I don't think you have any friends and so you made up this whole story to strike out at an innocent bystander, Sally, now didn't you?
Miss Smith:	That's not true!
Lawyer:	No further questions.
Miss Smith:	Ask Sally, she'll tell you!
Lawyer:	Self-incrimination? I think not!
Judge:	Step down, Miss Sm . . . , I mean Roxie. *(Miss Smith and the defense lawyer are seated.)*
Judge:	Bailiff, call the next witness.

Bailiff:	The court calls Mrs. Farkenparker. *(Mrs. Farkenparker stands in front of witness stand facing bailiff.)*
Bailiff:	Please raise your right hand. Do you promise to tell the truth, the whole truth, and nothing but the truth?
Mrs. Farkenparker:	I do.
Bailiff:	You may be seated.
Prosecutor:	*(Prosecutor approaches the witness.)* Mrs. Farkenparker, my first question to you is, do you have a first name that I may use to address you?
Mrs. Farkenparker:	Why yes, it's Hildegaard . . . but you may call me Hilda.
Prosecutor:	Thank goodness! *(relieved)* Hilda, I believe we have met once before, haven't we?
Mrs. Farkenparker:	Yes, we have.
Prosecutor:	Would you mind telling the court under what conditions that we last met?
Mrs. Farkenparker:	It was here in court.
Prosecutor:	Yes, it was here in court but on that day *you* were sitting where the accused are now and for the *exact same crime*—Christianity! Now, you being knowledgeable about this Christianity and all, you of all people should be able to tell a real Christian. Isn't that true?
Mrs. Farkenparker:	Well, yes, that is true.
Prosecutor:	And no doubt by now, after having spent some time in prison for this crime, you know what consequences face those who are guilty of Christianity, correct?
Mrs. Farkenparker:	Yes, that's correct.
Prosecutor:	So then, Hilda, tell us of your relationship to these two young people. *(points to defendants)*
Mrs. Farkenparker:	When we were able to have church and Sunday school, I was one of Sally and Mike's teachers.
Prosecutor:	You taught them this Christian faith, did you?
Mrs. Farkenparker:	I sure did and I'm proud of it!
Prosecutor:	Tell the truth now, did either of these two respond favorably to your teaching about God?
Mrs. Farkenparker:	Yes, they both did. Sally and Mike were very good students of the Bible.

Prosecutor:	Did either of them ever accept these teachings, or should I say in your lingo, "get saved?"
Mrs. Farkenparker:	Yes, they both did in my class one Sunday, I'm happy to say.
Prosecutor:	Your witness. *(Prosecutor returns to seat. Defense lawyer approaches the witness.)*
Lawyer:	Well, Mrs. Farkenparker, uh, Hilda, you seem not to care at all about what happens to these former pupils of yours. You say they are Christians knowing full well that they, too, could end up in prison like you have.
Mrs. Farkenparker:	I don't want them hurt but I do want them to know that it's no crime to stand up for Jesus and be counted. And whatever this court does to them is so small when compared with the crown they gain for being loyal to Christ. *(Mrs. F. looks at defendants and continues.)* Don't you kids ever deny Christ!
Lawyer:	Well, Hilda, since you're so versed in Christianity, why don't you tell us what a real Christian is like, and then we can have this court decide *if* these clients of mine are Christians or not. Go ahead, Hilda, tell us what a Christian is.
Mrs. Farkenparker:	A Christian is a person who receives Christ as the Savior and Lord of their life and dedicates their life to doing what the Bible says. This person is a truly happy Christian.
Lawyer:	A Christian then makes a personal *and* public commitment to Christ and his ways, correct?
Mrs. Farkenparker:	Correct.
Lawyer:	Would you say then that Mike exemplifies what a Christian is and does?
Mrs. Farkenparker:	*(mumbles)* Well, . . .
Lawyer:	I'm sorry, Hilda, we can't hear you.
Mrs. Farkenparker:	Well, I'm not sure.
Lawyer:	You're not sure? Hilda, this is a court of law and you're not sure?
Mrs. Farkenparker:	Well, he was once, but I don't know where he stands with the Lord now.
Lawyer:	From your own testimony you say that a Christian does what the Bible says, and the previous witnesses all claim that this is *not* the case with Mike. You defined Christianity; you make the judgment. Is Mike a Christian?

Prosecutor:	Objection. She's leading the witness.
Judge:	Overruled. Answer the question, Mrs. Farkenparker.
Mrs. Farkenparker:	I can't judge Mike, only God can.
Lawyer:	I take that as a definite no—Mike is not a Christian. He is innocent of the charge. I would also say that Sally is not guilty of being a Christian. No further questions. *(Lawyer returns to seat.)*
Mrs. Farkenparker:	Not so fast! Sally *I know* is serving God with all her heart!
Judge:	You may step down, Hilda. *(to prosecutor and lawyer)* Is that all the witnesses?
Prosecutor:	Yes, Your Honor.
Lawyer:	Yes, Your Honor.
Judge:	May the court hear your closing statements, please.
Prosecutor:	*(stands and paces while speaking)* Your Honor, after hearing the testimonies of our three witnesses, I'm sure you will readily agree that these two *(points at defendants)* are definitely guilty of First-degree Christianity.

In the case of Sally, we have heard an overwhelming volume of proof that she not only professes publicly and without reservation that she is a Christian but that she also lives out what she professes. Her honesty and moral convictions have been testified to by Mr. Jones, her boss. Her love for unlovable people has been testified to by Miss Smith. And her love for God and the Bible has been shown through Mrs. Farkenparker's testimony. What more can be said?

In regard to Mike, my gut feeling is that he is a master of disguise. I think the testimonies have shown vividly his attempts to hide his Christianity. He goes to church and embraces the teachings of Christ, but in everyday life he is like a chameleon—no one can tell by his words or actions that he is a Christian! He, your Honor, is guilty as well!

Lawyer:	*(Prosecutor is seated. Defense lawyer stands.)* Your Honor, to convict my two clients of Christianity would be an obvious breech of justice. The testimony shows clearly that neither Mike or Sally have Christian tendencies.

The testimony shows without question that Mike, even if he claimed to be a Christian, would be the worst example of a Christian. He doesn't profess publicly to be one, he doesn't act like one and that's because he's not one!

I'll admit, the evidence against Sally looks bad, but I'm sure that you'll agree that she is not responsible for her actions. She obviously has been brainwashed by people like Mrs. Farkenparker and others. No *sane* person would stand up and claim to be a Christian knowing full well that they would be punished for it. She's innocent by reason of insanity.

Sally:	*(Sally stands abruptly.)* Wait a minute! Can I say something now?
Lawyer:	Sit down and be quiet! The insanity plea is your only chance!
Judge:	*(pounds gavel)* Order! Let the defendant speak if she wishes.
Lawyer:	*(moves to seat while mumbling to Sally)* You've done it now, kid. You're on your own.
Sally:	*(Lawyer is seated. Sally moves toward judge.)* I'm not crazy and I'm not brainwashed. The only crazy thing I've done is allow her *(points to defense lawyer)* to represent me! Your Honor, everything that has been said about me by Mr. Jones, Roxie, and Mrs. Farkenparker is true. *I am a Christian* and whatever price I have to pay for it, I'm willing.
Lawyer:	Sally, I hope you like harmonica music 'cuz where you're going you'll hear lots of it.
Sally:	I don't care! Your Honor, the only important thing in life is serving Jesus. He died for us! Going to jail seems a small price to pay in return for the salvation he gives to us. You need Jesus too, Your Honor.
Lawyer:	*(sarcastically)* Great! Now she's witnessing to the judge!
Judge:	Is that all you wish to say, Sally?
Sally:	Yes, Your Honor.
Judge:	After hearing all the testimonies, I shall now decide the fate of these two young people.
Mike:	*(stands up nervously)* Your Honor!
Judge:	Yes, Mike? You wish to speak?
Mike:	Yes, I would.
Lawyer:	Sit down, they'll never convict you!

Mike: *(to lawyer)* I have to speak up. *(approaches judge)* Your Honor, the testimonies you've heard regarding me have also been true. I *do* go to church and I *do* claim to be a Christian. I guess I've been more concerned about what my friends think than about what God thinks. Yes, I'm a Christian, too, and whatever punishment there is, I'm willing to suffer, too. *(hangs head)*

Judge: *(Both Sally and Mike are now facing the judge.)* I am now ready to make my judgment. Sally, you are definitely guilty of being a Christian and the laws of this land dictate that you be imprisoned for not less than ten years. We cannot have your kind in our society . . . it's far too dangerous an influence.

Mike, *(Mike looks at the judge.)* I find you innocent of the charge of Christianity. There is absolutely no reason why this court or anyone else should think of you as a Christian. I don't know why you suddenly claimed to be a Christian today. *(laughingly)* Son, you're no more a Christian than I am!

Bailiff, take Sally away! This court is now closed. *(bangs the gavel as bailiff takes Sally away)*

Mike: *(Everyone leaves the courtroom except Mike who waits a moment, then turns to the audience.)* I don't believe it, my sister going to prison for being a Christian. Sally's a Christian through and through, everybody knows that. But prison? And here I stand, innocent. I should be happy but I feel sick inside. I'm a Christian, too, I thought.

What hurts me the most is this single thought: If this court can't find enough evidence to prove I'm a Christian, will Jesus be able to? *(turns and leaves)*

(lights out)

THE OFFERING SKIT

This short skit is a humorous way to introduce the subject of "giving." It could be used right before your next offering. You might want to follow it up with a short lesson on the proper way to give.

Characters: Three people who work together, but who attend three different churches.

#1: Boy, I'm sure glad it's payday. I've got a lot of bills to pay this week.

#2: Yeah, me too. I sure could use a raise. Then I could give more to the church. Right now, I can't hardly give any!

#3: Me neither. By the way, guys, how do you decide how much to give to God and how much to keep for yourself?

#1: Well, first I cash my paycheck. Then I draw a circle on the ground and throw all my money up into the air. Whatever lands inside the circle is God's. What lands outside the circle is mine.

#2: Oh really? Well, I do just the opposite. I draw a circle on the ground *(draws a large imaginary circle on the floor)*, throw all my money up in the air, and what lands *outside* the circle is God's; *inside* the circle, I keep.

#3: Well, I do it a little differently. I don't draw a circle at all. I throw all my money up in the air, and whatever God wants, he takes. Whatever comes back down, that's mine.

OH GOD!

This skit deals with the issue of "taking the name of the Lord in vain." It could also be tied in with a discussion of language in general.

(Two women are seated at a tennis match. Their heads are moving together watching the ball go back and forth. A player misses, the 1st woman speaks, and the heads stop moving temporarily.)

1st Woman:	Oh God, he missed the same shot twice in a row.
2nd Woman:	Oh, you talk to him, too?
1st Woman:	Huh? I wasn't talking to the player.
2nd Woman:	I know that. I meant God. Didn't I just hear you talk to him?
1st Woman:	Are you crazy? I don't even know the guy.
2nd Woman:	You just said, "Oh, God."
1st Woman:	That's just an expression. Be quiet and watch the match. *(Heads move again.)*
2nd Woman:	*(Heads stop.)* Oh Susie, *(as if swearing)* he should have had that.
1st Woman:	What? Who are you talking to?
2nd Woman:	Nobody. It's just an expression.
1st Woman:	What's the matter with you?
2nd Woman:	If you use God's name to swear by, can't I use someone else's name? In fact, I'll use your name next time.
1st Woman:	You can't do that!
2nd Woman:	Why not?
1st Woman:	'Cause . . . because it's just plain stupid! That's why!
2nd Woman:	*(pointing to match)* Here we go again. *(Heads move, then stop.)* Oh, Cindish darn it! *(swearing)* Did you see that?
1st Woman:	What did you say?
2nd Woman:	Cindish darn it. You know, like gosh darn it. Only I changed the name.
1st Woman:	But you can't use *my* name.
2nd Woman:	Why not? You use God's name.
1st Woman:	That's different!
2nd Woman:	What do you mean? You don't even know him and you use his name as an "expression." But I use your name and you get upset.
1st Woman:	This is ridiculous. If I had known you were such a religious fanatic, I wouldn't have asked you to come along.
2nd Woman:	O.K., Cindy, I'm sorry. I just get tired of people using my God's name as a silly expression to swear by. What if I used your dad's name or the name of someone you loved every time I cursed? You would think I was making fun of them. You see, I love God and I don't like people poking fun at him or his name. Besides, if you keep calling his name he might answer back.
1st Woman:	I think I can see what you're saying.

2nd Woman:	Hey, how about I go get us both something to drink?
1st Woman:	Sounds good! *(2nd Woman leaves, 1st Woman begins watching match with head moving, then stops.)* He lost the set. Oh God!
Voice over PA:	You called?

OOPS!

This skit takes a good-natured "dig" at archaeology. It can be used as a fun way to get into the subject of creation or to point out how we often distort facts to suit our own preconceived ideas about things.

Characters:	First Archaeologist
	Second Archaeologist
	Girl
	Prehistoric Man

Scene: There is a MAN lying on a table, flat on his back and covered with a blanket. Two archaeologists work near him, chiseling and digging. One chisels at the blanket and uncovers the man's toes.

First: Hey! I think I found something. Look at this!

Second: *(examines toes)* What do you think it is?

First: Must be some type of bone structure. Perhaps a claw or a hand of some prehistoric creature.

Second: How do we know it's prehistoric?

First: Because of these rock formations. We're working in a layer of prehistoric sediment.

Second: How do we know it's a prehistoric sediment?

First: Because the fossils we found here are prehistoric.

Second: How do we know these fossils are prehistoric?

First: Because we found them in this layer of prehistoric sediment!

Second: Ohhhhhh! *(puzzling)*

First: Let's see if there's more. *(They work together to uncover the legs up to the knees. They examine the legs closely.)*

Second: Those are the grossest looking hands and arms I've ever seen!

First: Do you think we've found it?

Second: *(excited)* It? *(puzzling)* What's "it"?

First: The missing link! The evolutionary connection between man and ape.

Second: Perhaps we should date these bones.

First: Excellent idea. I'll get the dater. *(exits and returns talking to a spacy GIRL)* Here it is, over here. We want you to date this.

Girl: I'll have to ask my mom first. She doesn't let me date strangers.

First: We want you to tell us how old it is.

Girl: Well, O.K., but I'm just doing it as a friend. Don't expect any kind of relationship to come from this.

Second: Look at these huge claws.

Girl: Yeah, they could use a trim. *(feeling legs and feet, looking them over)* I think I've dated this guy before.

Second: So what do you think?

Girl: Boy, I don't know. I'd say he's about nineteen . . . maybe twenty-one.

First: Twenty-one? He's gotta be over a million!

Girl: I'm sorry. This is only my third date.

First: I'd say he's about twenty-two million, give or take a century.

Second: That fits my theory.

First: Then that's what he is. Write it down. I'll keep working. *(While SECOND writes in a notebook, FIRST chisels the sheet away to uncover the entire MAN.)*

Girl: I know I've dated this guy before.

First: No wonder those hands are so ugly—they're feet.

Second: He looks a bit younger now, doesn't he?

First: We could adjust our theory, bring it down to about ten million.

Second: I can live with that.

Girl: I could never live with him. I can't even believe I dated him.

Second: What shall we name him?

Girl: See what it says on his I.D. tag.

First: I.D. tag?

Second: Here, around his neck. *(reading tag)* Captain I. M. Young, United States Army. *(pause)* Guess that blows our theory.

First: Wait a minute. *(thinking)* We can still save the theory somehow. Maybe explain away the I.D. tag—some kind of catastrophe or freak accident.

Girl: Freak is the word.

Second: I'm sure we could. We've done it before.

First: *(exiting with FIRST)* Let's take a look at my books. There must be something in there about prehistoric I.D. tags.

Girl: *(She studies MAN carefully, then glances to see if anyone's looking. She takes a slip of paper, writes on it quickly, and places it in the man's hand.)* Here's my number. I'm free Friday night.

PALM SUNDAY IN THE NEWS

This skit presents the events of Palm Sunday as if they were being covered by a television news team.

Characters:	Anchorperson Reporter Donkey Owner Crowd Member Chief Priest
Anchor:	*(The anchorperson could be sitting at a desk to one side with call letters, microphone, etc.)* This is a Jerusalem Network News Special Report with your WGOD anchorperson, _____, covering today's startling events on the Bethphage Road. And now to our reporter, _____.
Reporter:	We're here on the Bethphage Road where quite a large crowd has gathered to cheer the arrival of a man we've all been hearing about recently, Jesus of Nazareth. You can hear in the background the shouts of ''Hosanna'' and ''Blessed is he who comes in the name of the Lord'' and even ''Blessed is the King of Israel.'' Although we've had prophets before whom the crowds have hailed as king, the arrival of this one is a little unique because he's shunned the normal white horse or black stallion routine, and he's riding to Jerusalem on the back of a small donkey. We have here a man who is personally involved in this parade. Will you tell our viewing audience what part you have in all this commotion?
Donkey Owner:	Sure! Do you see the man in the white robe everyone is yelling at? Well, he's that prophet from Nazareth that's been showing up everywhere preaching and doing miracles.
Reporter:	And how are you involved with him?
Donkey Owner:	Well, you might say that without me this whole parade wouldn't be happening at all! See that? He's riding *my* donkey.
Reporter:	Oh, do you rent them?
Donkey Owner:	No, he's a family pet. Great animal. A little small, but big on dependability.
Reporter:	Uh, to get back to the prophet . . .
Donkey Owner:	Oh yeah. There were, my donkey and me, standing inside the Bethphage Gate minding our own business, when these two guys come up

and start untying her. Well I says, "Just what do you think you're doing with my animals, you clowns?"

And they says to me, "The Lord needs it and will send it back here shortly."

Well for some reason I just stood there and let them take her. I don't understand it—I mean, two strangers take my donkey right out from under my nose and I say, "Sure go ahead." It ain't like me at all.

Reporter:	Thank you, Sir, and good luck with getting your donkey back again.
Donkey Owner:	Yeah, thanks, it just ain't like me at all. (*walks away shaking his head*)
Reporter:	Let's see if we can talk to a member of this crowd here. Uh, ma'am, could you come over here a minute please?
Crowd Member:	Who me? You mean me?
Reporter:	Yes, I'd like you to describe for our viewers just why it is that you're here today.
Crowd Member:	Hey, I make it to all these Hosanna Parades. I've seen more prophets, messiahs, and saviors come and go than your average Tom, Dick, or Judas.
Reporter:	Do you think this one is just like all the others?
Crowd Member:	Well, if the stories are true, this guy could be someone special. I mean there's a rumor that he actually *raised someone from the dead* not long ago over in Bethany. If that's true, this may not be your average messiah. I mean, I wouldn't go so far as to say he's really, well, you know, but every now and then you have to wonder if just maybe the real thing might not show up and do in the Romans.
Reporter:	And if you thought this Jesus really were the "real thing," what do you think you'd do about it?
Crowd Member:	I'm not saying I'd do anything. You gotta go with the flow. You know how these crowds are—"Hosanna" today, "Crucify him" tomorrow. I'm not sure they really want much to do with an actual messiah. Who knows what they might do to one?
Reporter:	Yes, thank you. That's an interesting point of view. Oh, look! We're in luck. One of the chief priests is heading this way. Maybe we can get a word with him. Excuse me . . . excuse me, Sir, do you have a minute to share an official opinion about what's going on here today?

Chief Priest:	Yes, we've prepared a statement for the press. Ahem. *(reads)* We have been carefully monitoring the movements of this Jesus of Nazareth, and we find his attitude and his claims to border on blasphemy. We'd advise the faithful Jews who are listening to take care lest they be led astray.
Reporter:	But Sir, what do you think of the alleged miracles and—
Chief Priest:	That's all I have to say. *(walks away)*
Reporter:	Oh! Well, sure, thank you. And now back to you, _____ (anchor).
Anchor:	Well, as you can see, everyone is rather noncommittal as to who this Jesus of Nazareth really is, although the fervor here today would lead you to believe that he has a lot of support of some sort.
	I guess we'll all have to wait and see the results of his stay in Jerusalem this Passover week and make our own decisions. Just who do *you* think he is? *(pause)* This is _____ reporting. Good day.

PARABLE OF THE SHAPES

This skit is excellent for use in conjunction with a discussion on the subject of love. It is based on the idea that there are basically three kinds of love: "if" love, "because" love, and "in-spite-of" love (the best kind, of course).

Characters:	Narrator
	1st Circle
	2nd Circle
	Blob
	1st Star
	2nd Star
	1st Square
	2nd Square
	1st Triangle
	2nd Triangle
	In-Spite-Of Man

The characters should each carry a large cardboard shape as their costume. Their identities thus become their shapes; for example, the Blob should carry a cardboard shape that is uneven and rather nondescript, and the In-Spite-Of man should carry no shape at all.

Narrator:	There once was a land of If and Because
	That sat on the earth as every land does.
	And every person who lived in the land
	Would search for a person he could understand
	Now let us together observe what takes place
	When If and Because people meet face-to-face.
1st Circle:	As I walk along this fine sunny day,
	A stranger I see coming my way.
	Is he a friend or is he a foe?
	Not till I look at his shape will I know.
	A circle I be and a circle I stay.
	A circle is needed for friendship today.
	(enter the Blob) Hello my friend, Circle's my name
	And finding a friend is my kind of game
	Have you a circle to exchange with me here?
	Or are you an alien shape, I fear?
Blob:	A friendly fellow you seem to be
	And circles I need for good friends to be.
	What my own shape is, I really don't know
	But I hope it's a circle so friendship will grow.
	I'm so glad I found you, I'm so glad to see
	That such a relationship can possibly be.
1st Circle:	Now wait a minute, oh stranger here.
	You hasten your happiness too fast I fear.
	I told you before our two shapes must match
	In order for any new friendship to hatch.
	If you were a circle with roundest of frame,
	We'd be friends forever because we're the same.
	But I see no circle, I see nothing round.

I think that it's only a Blob that I've found,
Now think of my image, what others might say,
I can't take the risk. Away! Away!

Blob:
I'm so broken-hearted, I'm in such despair.
I am not a circle. It doesn't seem fair. *(enter 2nd Circle)*

2nd Circle:
A call for a circle, is that what I hear?
I, too, am a circle, such joy and such cheer!
For now, brother Circle, your long vigil ends.
We've found one another. Forever we're friends! *(Two Circles embrace and walk off.)*

1st Star:
I am a star, a beautiful star.
Better than all other shapes, by far.
And if you are the finest, I think you will see
That shape you are holding, a star it will be.
If I'd find a star, we'd frolic in fun

And dance and play and never be done.
If you are a star, my friendship you've won.
But as I look closer, I see you're not one.
You're only a Blob! We'll never go far,
Unless you can prove that you're also a star!

Blob: My shape's not important. Myself is what counts.
Just give me some friendship in any amount.

1st Star: I've no time for Blobs, so go on your way,
For I think a star is coming this way. (enter 2nd Star)

2nd Star: A star I am, and a star I'll stay.
Oh praise be to stars, it's our lucky day!

1st Star: Oh star, oh star, what double delight!
These shapes that we're holding, they match us just right.

2nd Star: At last we're together, so happy and proud.
Together we'll surely stand out in a crowd.
So Blob, adios! Farewell and good-by!
You just don't fit in, and don't ask us why.

Blob:	Alas, I am broken. What worse could I do?
	Than being rejected by each of these two. *(enter 1st Square)*
1st Square:	Through this crowd I now will stare
	To see if perhaps there be somewhere a square.
	Pardon me there, but some time could you lend?
	If you are a square, I'll be your true friend.
Blob:	Oh surely, dear brother, our shape's not the same,
	But I'm a sweet person, and what's in a name?
1st Square:	Your shape's not a square and you talk to me so?
	I can't believe all the nerve that you show.
	If it's friendship you want, then friendship go get.
	But not from a shape with which you don't fit! *(enter 2nd Square)*
2nd Square:	A call for a square? I'll soon be right there!
	A square I am and a square I'll be.
	I'll join you in friendship, oh square, just ask me.
	Because our fine corners do each number four,
	We'll stay close together forever and more! *(They both exit.)*
Blob:	I'm torn and I'm frazzled, what worse could there be,
	Than being rejected by each of these three. *(enter 1st Triangle)*
1st Triangle:	I'm wandering to and I'm wandering fro,
	In search of a three-sided shape just like so. *(points)*
	For if I could find one, I know we would blend,
	For only a triangle can be a true friend.
Blob:	Hello there, dear fellow, I've heard all you've said,
	I can't help but thinking, to you I've been led.
	For you need friendship and I need the same.
	So on with the friendship and off with the game.
1st Triangle:	Now who is this talking? What shape do you hold?
	You seem sort of strange, just what is your mold?
	You sure are not pretty, you shapeless disgrace.
	Why, you're just a Blob, it's all over your face!
	I've no time for you, you pitiful one.
	This senseless discussion is over and done! *(enter 2nd Triangle)*

2nd Triangle:	A call for triangles? Well I'll fill the need.
	We're made for each other, it must be agreed! *(They exit together.)*
Blob:	No one understands poor shapeless me,
	Cause I'm just a Blob as you can well see.
	If I were a circle or maybe a square,
	Then I could be having some fun over there.
	Why can't all you shapes just notice and see,
	That I'm just as miserable as I can be.
	With no one to laugh and be good friends with,
	I'm beginning to feel just a little bit miffed.
Narrator:	Now just at this moment comes into this place
	A man who is different in style and in grace.
	He's quiet and thoughtful and listens quite well,
	Observing the stories that our characters tell.
	Now with me return to our tale if you can,
	And witness the ways of In-Spite-Of Man. *(enter In-Spite-Of Man)*
In-Spite-Of Man:	Hello, will you be my friend?
Blob:	Oh, no, can't you see . . .
	I'm not a circle or square, so please leave me be.
In-Spite-Of Man:	Friend, once again to you I will say,
	Will you not be my friend on this fine day?
Blob:	Your humor's not funny. I'm wise to your jokes.
	You're here to make fun like the rest of these folks.
In-Spite-Of Man:	Now what is the problem, my poor little man?
	You seem so distressed, I just can't understand.
Blob:	I've run the whole gamut, I've pleaded and cried
	To have them accept me and love me inside.
	But each time I seek them, they look at my shape,
	And quickly reject me, it's like hearing a tape.
	"You're not the right person, you've got the wrong shape,
	The people will gossip, the people will gape."
	If this shall continue from day unto day,
	Alone I'll remain and depressed will I stay.

In-Spite-Of Man:	I think a great lesson's been brought to your sight.
	These shapes find it hard to accept you "in spite."
	They're all so possessive and selfish inside,
	They wallow in vanity, ego, and pride.
	But there is an answer I've found to be true,
	And I've come to offer this answer to you.
Blob:	I don't understand all you're trying to say,
	But you're the first person I've met here today
	Who seems to accept me in spite of my form
	You break all the rules of the shape-seekers' norm.
In-Spite-Of Man:	Your wisdom is growing, I think you now see
	Love puts no conditions on you or on me.

Narrator:	Our moral is simple, I'll share it with you.
	It's all in the Bible and known to be true.
	The world offers values, which dazzle our eyes,
	It mixes the truth with ridiculous lies.
	And we here are seeking the true meaning of
	This life that we're living, this word we call "love."
	The If and Because folks are caught in a bind,
	For they only accept their very own kind.
	They love folks "because" and they love people "if,"
	But few have discovered the "In-Spite-Of" Gift!

THE SACRIFICE

Here's a short skit that is an example of how to interpret creatively a Scripture passage to a group. Based on Romans 12:1–2, this skit should be memorized and rehearsed by the participants to maximize communication. You might try creating similar skits based on other familiar passages, or allow the kids in your group to write their own as part of a Bible study.

Person #1: I beg of you, Christian youth, because God is so merciful, present your body a living sacrifice—holy and acceptable to God. This is the reasonable way to serve him.

Person #2: Sacrifice! Sacrifice? When I think of sacrifice, I think of some pagan tribe in Africa. I see a live, wiggling body lying on a cold slab or rock. I see fire under the slab and the body burning as a sacrifice to an idol. You want me to be a sacrifice? Not me! I'm too young to die!

Person #1: Who said anything about dying? God wants you alive—a living sacrifice—that means to live for God, to serve and love him.

Person #2: Oh. That sounds a little better. (*pause*) But I don't know. It sounds like I'd have to give up a lot. I mean I really enjoy living—doing the things I want to do. You know what I mean?

Person #1: Yes, I know what you mean. But being a living sacrifice means a change of mind—you no longer want to do what you want to do, instead you want to do what God wants you to do.

Person #2: Wanting to do what God wants me to do instead of wanting to do what I want to do? That sounds like a lot of double-talk. *(pause)* Besides, I already don't really want to do what I want to do. Mostly I want to do what my friends want to do.

Person #1: Conformity?

Person #2: Huh?

Person #1: You are talking about conformity, aren't you? Your mind is set on conforming to the world's standards. Is that right?

Person #2: Yes, that's right. Huh? I mean, no, that's not right is it? I mean, it's what I mean, but it's not right.

Person #1: So you do know the difference?

Person #2: Of course. I *am* a Christian. I know the Bible says, "Be not conformed to this world." But it's very difficult not to be. You know what I mean?

Person #1: Sure. I have the same problem.

Person #2: You do?

Person #1: All Christians do. The pull of the world is very strong. Everything and everybody encourage us to conform. That is, everybody, *but* God who made us. He knows us so well that he knows conformity won't bring us happiness in our Christian life. That's why he tells us not to conform to the world but to be transformed.

Person #2: Transformed? That's a fancy word for changed, isn't it?

Person #1: Yes. God wants us to change and the only way we can change and become the living sacrifice he wants us to be is by putting our mind on him. When we look at God instead of at the world, our desire becomes to do the will of God.

Person #2: And the will of God is that we become living sacrifices?

Person #1: Say, you figure things out pretty fast.

Person #2: You know, when I think about it, it would be easier to become a dead sacrifice.

Person #1: How do you come up with that?

Person #2: Well, you'd only have to die one time and it would all be over. But this living sacrifice bit—it's so . . . so . . .

Person #1: Daily?

Person #2: You got it!

Person #1: But it's the only sacrifice that is acceptable to God.

Person #2: I really want to offer an acceptable sacrifice.

Person #1: Then you'll do it?

Person #2: Yes, I'll live for God each day of my life. I'll become a living sacrifice—no longer conformed to the world but transformed by putting my mind on God. After all, it's the only reasonable way to serve him.

Person #1: And the only way to prove what is the good, acceptable, and perfect will of God.

SAYIN', DOIN', OR BEIN'

The characters in this skit are two demons, one a little smarter than the other. The reference to the "Enemy" is to God, as in C. S. Lewis' *Screwtape Letters*.

Leo: *(Ernie is seated reading a newspaper. Leo rushes in.)* Ernie, Ernie, you gotta help me. I'm just about to lose a client.

Ernie: What do you mean? You've never lost a client.

Leo: I think I'm losin' my touch.

Ernie: Get ahold of yourself, Leo. You're not losin' it. You're one of the worst demons I know.

Leo: Really?

Ernie: Yeah. You're terrible! You're ugly! You're mean! You're nasty!

Leo: I am? I mean, I am. I'm a rotten, bad-for-nothin' demon.

Ernie: Now, go back out there and get 'em!

Leo: Right! *(goes out confidently, then comes right back in)* Wait a minute. I need some advice, Ernie.

Ernie: Sure, what is it?

Leo: See, I have this one client who's on the Enemy's side. I mean he really is on our side, but he claims to be a follower of the Enemy's Son. I taught him early that Christianity is only a lot of talk. You don't have to *do* anything, just *say* you're a follower of the Enemy.

Ernie: Sounds like you're doin' great.

Leo: I was for a while. I really had this guy—all talk and no action. I mean his faith was really shallow.

Ernie: What happened?

Leo:	He talked to some faithful followers of the Enemy. They got him started *doin'*, besides just talkin'. He's puttin' his faith into action.
Ernie:	Have you tried boostin' his ego by good deeds?
Leo:	Yeah! I'm tryin' to get him on a good-deed kick. You know, tryin' to earn his salvation by works.
Ernie:	Sounds like you got him to me. Just overemphasize the works, instead of the faith. He'll think he's a goody-two-shoes.
Leo:	But I keep thinkin' if he is doin' good things, the Enemy is gonna like him and I'll lose him.
Ernie:	You're not even close to losin' him yet. If you can get a human to say he is the Enemy's child but not act like it, he's comin' our way. If you can get him to do good deeds with the wrong motive, you still have him. But when he starts *bein'* instead of just doin' or sayin', then you got problems.
Leo:	What do you mean *bein'*?
Ernie:	*Bein'* a follower of the enemy. There's a lot of difference between sayin', doin', and bein'.
Leo:	You mean like some people say they follow the Enemy, some act like it, and some actually do it.
Ernie:	Right! The Enemy wants his followers not just to say or do certain things, but to *become* something—to become a faithful follower.
Leo:	So if I can keep this guy worried about sayin' or doin', he won't have time to become.
Ernie:	And as long as he keeps askin' questions like "Do I *have* to do this?" or "Is this really that bad?" then he still hasn't become a follower. But you gotta be careful to keep him from growin' up.
Leo:	Yeah, if his faith ever matured, I'd lose him.
Ernie:	Just never let what he's sayin' and doin' sink into his heart. That's what the Enemy wants—his heart. If his faith ever penetrates the surface, watch out because your fall is comin'.
Leo:	Now you got me scared again, Ernie.
Ernie:	You know, Leo, I'm kinda scared, too. I get scared just talkin' about the Enemy. *(Both exit.)*

THE $64,000 TESTIMONY

This skit deals with the topic of "clichés" and honesty in the Christian faith. It should be set up like a TV game show.

Characters: Announcer
               Buddy Barker
               Adelle Haggerty
               Judge #1
               Judge #2
               Judge #3
               Judge #4
               Aunty Ruth Goldenrod
               Barry Speerchucker

Announcer: It's the $64,000 Testimony! And now, here's the host of the $64,000 Testimony, Buddy Barker!

Barker: Thank you, thank you! You're too kind! Please hold the applause! Thank you. We've got a tremendous show for you with some stiff competition! See how well you match up with our judges as *we* rate the testimony of our first contestant, Adelle Haggerty! Welcome to our show, Adelle. Please step up to the microphone and give us the best testimony you've got!

Adelle: Thank you, Buddy. I'd like to tell you all that Jesus is all the world to me. Life with him is joy unspeakable and full of glory, full of glory, full of glory and the half of it has never yet been told. It's been my experience that Jesus never fails. What a friend I've had in Jesus since he loves me just as I am. Thank you.

Barker: Thank you, Adelle! Let's see how our judges respond. Judge #1, on a scale of one to ten, how do you rate Ms. Haggerty?

Judge #1: I gave her a 4, Buddy. No new material. Totally unoriginal.

Barker: Thank you. Judge #2.

Judge #2: I think churches are getting tired of clichés, Buddy. I'm sorry, but I gave her a 2.

Barker: Judge #3? Same answer?

Judge #3:	No, I put her down as average. She had a great Spirit, but little content. She gets a 5.
Barker:	And Judge #4?
Judge #4:	It's true that she used outdated phrases, but she communicated well. I liked her. I gave her an 8.
Barker:	O.K.—how about our next contestant! Aunty Ruth Goldenrod!
Aunty:	I accepted Christ when I was a child of four years, at which point I realized that my sin was making habitation for Satan. At four-and-a-half, I was sanctified wholly, forever being cleansed of Adam's original and depraved sin. My call to the mission field did not come until I was eight years old and thus ended the three-and-one-half years of trials and searching. I have served him unfailingly and without complaint since then. For I know my reward is in the life to come.
Barker:	Thank you, Aunty Ruth! Judges?
Judge #1:	Way beyond my attention span, Buddy. She could use some zip in her delivery! I gave her a 4.
Judge #2:	She raised some theologically unsound issues, Buddy. Issues I'm not sure she should be treating with her lack of credentials. Being sanctified at the age of four-and-one-half is virtually impossible. My son is eighteen and says he *still* hasn't reached the age of accountability! With all that in mind, I gave her a 3.
Barker:	What about you, Judge #3?
Judge #3:	It was an average missionary story. I think we all could have finished her sentences for her since she had nothing new to say. I gave her a 5.
Barker:	And Judge #4?
Judge #4:	I think you're being a little tough on her when you take into account that she's in her fifties, has never married, and probably lost touch with reality years ago. She tries hard, so I gave her an 8.
Barker:	I think our judges are being extra careful today! Keep in mind, you who are in our viewing audience, that this panel has heard thousands of testimonies, songs, prayers, pleas for money, and sermons. They were hand-picked by me for their vast experience. They're the best in the business, if I do say so. So, you have to do something pretty zany to tickle these fellows' ears! And speaking of zany, let's bring out our third contestant, Barry Speerchucker, who will be giving his testimony in song!

Barry:	Life—started out like a race track.
	The starting line covered with cars.
	With a word, we're all dodging and crashing,
	'till we reach the checkered flag in the stars.
Barker:	A creative approach indeed! Judges, how do you react? Let's start with Judge #4.
Judge #4:	His vibrato was good and singing without accompaniment like that takes guts and perfect pitch. I gave him a 7.
Barker:	O.K., Judge #3?
Judge #3:	It sounds to me like he could use a tune up. Ho! Ho! Seriously, though, the song had good emotional appeal but little eternal value. I gave him a 6 for musical ability.
Barker:	And Judge #2?
Judge #2:	The song was fine, but he really tried to force his personality on us. A real cheesy smile, you know. For that I gave him a 4.
Barker:	And Judge #1?
Judge #1:	Analogies are outdated, Buddy. That made it just under average, so I gave him a 4.
Barker:	Well, that's it for tonight. Our judges are tabulating the scores to see who our big winner is. The winner is—Oh! I can't believe it—the winner is Aunty Ruth Goldenrod! Congratulations, Aunty Ruth Goldenrod, you have won the $64,000 Testimony.
Aunty:	Oh! Oh! Oh! I am so excited! Oh, Praise the Lord! Oh, I'm so happy and here's the reason why!
Barker:	And what is the reason, Aunty?
Aunty:	What?
Barker:	I say, what is the reason you're so happy?
Aunty:	I don't know what you're talking about, smarty-pants.
Barker:	But Aunty Ruth Goldenrod, you just said, "I'm so happy and here's the reason why." So why are you so happy?
Aunty:	What are you? An intellectual or something? How do I know why? I just said it. I don't have to answer your tricky questions.
Barker:	Well, that's all the time we have, folks. Tonight's big winner of the $64,000 Testimony has been Aunty Ruth Goldenrod. Tune in again next week when we

will have three new contestants with three old testimonies that could just be the $64,000 Testimony!

SONGS OF THE HEART

This script is a simple yet thought-provoking drama that deals with the topic of worship and praise. The setting for this production is the stage of your church auditorium with the youth standing on risers. The story depicts a typical youth choir rehearsal that turns into a not-so-typical experience as the youth, with a little help from the Director and a Guest from the past, come to full awareness of the importance of their actions and attitudes when worshiping God.

The cast calls for eighteen speaking parts, though many can be combined, so that a group of eight to ten can just as easily present the drama. There is no need for elaborate costumes or props. Small items, such as horn-rimmed glasses for the *Brain* and a muscle T-shirt for the *Enforcer*, are sufficient to develop individual roles. The *Director, John Newton,* and the *Messenger* can be played by adults if necessary. In fact, the *Director* might most naturally be played by the actual choir director at your church. Adapt the script as necessary and use the real names of people in your group when appropriate.

Besides the dialogue, you will need to sing four hymns: "Amazing Grace," "It Is Well with My Soul," "Just As I Am," and "I Have Decided to Follow Jesus."

Characters: Choir Director
John Newton
Messenger
Class Clown
Brain
Enforcer
Mediator
Youth #1
Youth #2
Youth #3
Youth #4
Youth #5

Youth #6
Youth #7
Youth #8
Singer #1
Singer #2
Speaker

Scene #1: When the lights come on, the youth and Director are positioned on stage facing the audience. The Director gets the attention of the youth and begins to lead them in singing "Amazing Grace." The kids sing through the first verse of the hymn half-heartedly. As the youth choir starts the second verse, the *Director* becomes frustrated and speaks.

Director:	Wait a minute! Hold everything! That's the worst singing I've ever heard. We're supposed to be singing about amazing grace, but you all sound bored to tears. Let's try it again and get it right this time. Put some enthusiasm into your voices.
Messenger:	*(Messenger enters from the rear and calls out to the Director.)* _____, *(Director's name)*, you've got a phone call. I told them you were busy, but they said it was kinda important, so I put them on hold.
Director:	O.K., tell them I'll be right there. *(turning to the choir)* Now look, you guys, I've got to go answer the phone. I'm going to leave _____ *(Enforcer's name)*, in charge. *(general grumbling by the rest of the youth)* I want you to practice this song while I'm gone. I'm expecting some major improvement by the time I return.
Enforcer:	*(Director leaves and Enforcer steps forward.)* O.K., everyone, you heard what the man said. I'm in charge! Now we're going to sing this song and we're going to sing it right.
Clown:	*(stepping to the front while the Enforcer moves back in place)* That's right gang. Let's all sing this song, but let's do it the way I taught you. All together now, in the key of G.
Brain:	Excuse me, but you seem to have made a mistake! We never sing "Amazing Grace" in the key of G. In fact— *(interrupted)*
Youth #1:	He doesn't really mean the key of G. He means let's sing "Amazing Grace" to the tune of "Gilligan's Island." *(All youth cheer and sway back and forth when the singing begins.)*

Clown:	*(humming a pitch for choir and motioning with his arms)* All together now! *(Choir sings through first verse of "Amazing Grace" to the tune of "Gilligan's Island." When they start the second verse, they are interrupted by Newton.)*
Newton:	*(from a seat in the audience)* Wait a minute! That's not the way that song is supposed to be sung.
Youth #2:	*(sarcastically)* What do you mean? Those were the right words, weren't they?
Newton:	Yes, but you're still doing it all wrong.
Clown:	Well, isn't that the way Gilligan would have sung it?
Youth #3:	You know, he's got a point there!
Clown:	Why don't you two be quiet and listen to the man!
Newton:	Listen! You're missing the point. Sure, those are the right words, but even if you were singing the right tune, you would still be singing the song all wrong.
Brain:	Now wait a minute. That's completely illogical! If we were to put that in the form of a syllogism we— *(interrupted)*
Youth #4:	Look, I don't know what you're getting at, Mister, but what makes you such an expert on this song anyway? You sound like you think you wrote the song yourself.
Newton:	I did!
Youth #5:	*(sarcastically)* Sure you did! We believe you. *(to group)* We do believe him, don't we? *(general mocking agreement by all youth)*
Clown:	*(looks to the audience and begins to circle the side of his head with his finger, signifying that Newton is crazy)*
Newton:	Listen! My name is John Newton and I wrote the song that you guys are *not* singing. I say you're *not* singing it because you've left out the most important part. You see, when I wrote that song, I meant it to be an expression of my faith and commitment to God. His grace was truly amazing to me. When I sang that song, it was a way of worship, but when you sing it, you don't seem to give a thought to what you're actually saying. My song has lasted all these years because it expresses the gratitude of the countless people who sing it. So you see, though you sing the right words and keep my tune, unless you sing my song from your heart to God, you're not really singing it the way I had hoped it would always be sung.

Scene #2: Newton exits as the choir members murmur among themselves. Newton is passed by the Director who now reenters.

Director:	Well guys, I'm sorry for that short delay. I hope you've practiced the song and you're ready to give it your best effort. *(Director motions for all to stand properly. The choir reacts silently and sings "Amazing Grace" soulfully.)*
Director:	Now that's more like it! I don't know what inspired you guys, but let's keep up the good work. *(pause)* Now, let's sing our second song "It Is Well with My Soul."
Youth #6:	Hey, I know that song! It's got something to do with some man who lost his entire family, all his friends, and his life savings in a combined earthquake and flood. Then he himself came down with this dreaded disease or something that made him unable to run, jump, or play. Isn't that right, _____ ? *(Director's name)*
Director:	Well not exactly. Actually— *(interrupted)*
Brain:	As a point of fact, *(looking to Director)* if I may be so bold, *(Director nods approval)* that song was written by Horatio G. Spafford— *(interrupted)*
Clown:	*(looking to audience)* Oh Horatio, are *you* out there?
Brain:	*(with disgusted look on his face)* As I was saying, that song was written by Mr. Spafford while standing aboard a ship that had arrived at the location where Mr. Spafford's two daughters drowned just days before his arrival. As he looked down into the water, in the midst of his sorrow, he was inspired to write "It is Well with My Soul."
Youth #7:	*(speaking to director)* Is that true?
Director:	Yes, it is true. Perhaps that's one of the reasons why that song has meant so much to so many people. Understanding why a song was written can really help you appreciate it. Don't you agree? *(general agreement)*
Director:	Well then, let's give this song a try. *(Director motions with his arms, and the choir sings three verses of "It is Well with My Soul.")*
Youth #8:	Wow, that's a great song! _____ *(Director's name)*, are there any other songs we sing in church that have interesting stories behind them?
Director:	Sure, lots of them do. In fact, the song we're going to sing next has an interesting story. Does anyone know the story behind "Just as I Am"?

Brain:	I do!
Clown:	Anybody else?
Enforcer:	Pipe down and listen to the man.
Mediator:	Easy you two! Let's not forget why we're here in the first place.
Director:	That's right! _____ *(Brain's name),* go ahead and tell us about "Just As I Am."
Brain:	Well, O.K. The song was written by a woman named Charlotte Elliott. She was badly crippled and struggled with a tremendous feeling of self-worthlessness. Well, one day a preacher talked to her and told her that God loved her just as she was.
Youth #3:	And that's what inspired her to write the song?
Director:	That's right. Now let's sing it. *(Choir sings "Just As I Am.")*
Youth #1:	That's a great song, too. I've sung these songs for years and years now, but this is the first time I've ever really stopped to think about what I was singing. *(general group agreement)*
Youth #2:	Me, too, and I'll bet there are a lot of other people just like us. We all get so used to singing the same old songs over and over and over and— *(interrupted)*
Enforcer:	We get the point!
Youth #4:	Yea, but do we get the message?
Youth #7:	*(speaking to Youth #4)* What do you mean?
Youth #4:	Well, it's like, we always sing these quote, unquote, "Great Hymns of the Faith." Yet, we don't really seem to live the message that we sing. Take, for example, the song "Stand Up For Jesus."
Youth #5:	Oh, I hate that song! That's the one where they always make you stand up just to sing it. Then everyone stands there hoping that they'll only have to sing the first verse.
Clown:	Are you suggesting we sing, "Sit Down, Sit Down for Jesus"?
Youth #5:	No! We need to stand up for Jesus. I just hate to stand up for "Stand Up For Jesus."
Mediator:	Personally, I don't really mind standing while singing that song. I think of it as sorta acting out the ideas of the song. Though sometimes I feel like a hypocrite because I know I don't always stand up for Jesus like I should.
Youth #4:	That's what *I* was trying to say!

Youth #8:	The song that really makes me feel like a hypocrite is "I Surrender All." _____ (Director's name), how do you think God feels when we sing a song like "I Surrender All" when he knows we really haven't?
Director:	I don't really know, but I'm sure our careless and thoughtless approach to our singing can't be the kind of worship that God wants. I'm certain it's not what he deserves!
Enforcer:	That's right! What's even worse though is the way some of the people in *this* youth group act while they're supposed to be singing. Just last Sunday I was sitting in the back and I heard two "young people" talking during the invitation hymn. We had just finished the first verse when . . . *(Voice fades and lights black out to set up for upcoming skit.)*

Scene #3: In the darkness, the choir softly sings a couple verses of "I Have Decided" while Singer #1 and #2 slip into place at the front of the stage. The lights return to find Singer #1 and #2 together as if in the last row of the auditorium during the singing of an invitation hymn.

Singer #1:	Excuse me! Did you happen to catch the page number of the song we're supposed to be singing?
Singer #2:	No, I'm afraid I didn't, but I wouldn't worry about it if I were you. The song will be over in a couple of minutes.
Singer #1:	I know, but I feel strange standing here doing nothing while everyone else is singing. I mean, it's kinda embarrassing!
Singer #2:	Well, you can always do what I do.
Singer #1:	What's that?
Singer #2:	Just look pious and move your mouth as if you were actually singing the song.
Singer #1:	You do that?
Singer #2:	Sure! It's easy. Just watch the preacher's mouth. When he opens his mouth, you open yours. When he closes his mouth, you close yours. There's really nothing to it, and everyone thinks you're singing all the while.
Singer #1:	Shh! The preacher is looking at us. *(Both begin to mouth the words to the song that the choir is softly singing behind them.)* Hey, that works great!

Singer #2:	Sure, and for extra fun you can always move your mouth as if you're singing, but make up new words as you go. It's a great way to pass the time while you're waiting for the service to end. *(A blackout while the Singers return to their places and, when the lights come back on, the Enforcer is continuing his comments.)*
Enforcer:	Frankly, I was shocked! I— *(interrupted)*
Mediator:	If the truth were known, I guess we've all been more than a little careless in our worship. I don't think we've really stopped to think how important it is to God that we worship him wholeheartedly—not just when we're singing, but in every part of our lives. I remember hearing in Bible school that the ideas of worship and service both often come from the same word in the Bible. Our entire lives should be lived worshipfully and as a servant. I just pray that God will help all of us be more sincere and consistent in every part of our lives.
Speaker:	*(closing remarks to audience)* Every Sunday we come here to this building and sing songs of worship and praise. Some of the songs we sing were written by men and women of faith who suffered greatly; others were written by those who sought to express their devotion to God and to their Savior; still others were written to teach or encourage the church. These "Great Hymns of the Faith" have not lasted so long because of their witty lyrics or elaborate tunes, but because they express the heart of a people driven to worship by the majesty of their God.
	When we lift our voices to sing, we must never forget to whom we are singing. We must not simply echo thoughtless phrases mastered during childhood or painfully render a half-hearted effort while longing for the song to end. We are not just singing; we are worshiping. In worship your attitude counts! Your words should rise up from you as a musical prayer or as a powerful declaration of what you hold to be true. For great is our Lord and greatly to be praised!

THE SPONTANEOUS SAMARITAN

This is a "spontaneous" skit, where actors are randomly pulled from the audience with no knowledge of what they are to do until they hear the narrator read the script. Each person is assigned a part, and the only instruction is to do what the script calls for him to do.

One day a goodly traveler was trucking along humming to himself, thinking everything was fine, when all of a sudden out of the rocks jumped three of the meanest gangsters you've ever seen. They had beady eyes and they ground their teeth together. They started to beat on the traveler, then all at once two of them grabbed his arms while the other started to punch him. When the action seemed to freeze, then the traveler remembered and said to himself, "I know Kung Fu!" And he broke free and started to fight back. But the gangsters knocked him down to the ground. *(Chances are he is already on the ground, but repeat the words "But on the way down" until he gets up.)* But on the way down to the ground, he let out a loud and terrible shout, followed by a deep grunt. The thieves grabbed his money and split, yelling and leaping for joy.

As he lay there, groaning and groaning, along came a priest who, seeing the man, was shocked. The priest walked around him and said, "I am shocked but it serveth him righteth, for traveling aloneth."

Then came a Levite, and the man is still groaning. When the Levite saw and heard him, he ran to the side of the man and said, "Oh my, oh my, what a pity!" And he started to help the man up but then noticed what time it was and dropped the man. The man let out a scream. The Levite said, "I am lateth for worship at the synagogueth, must not let man come before God." And he walked away.

And finally came along a Samaritan who, after seeing the man, was moved with compassion and came over to bandage the man, then helped him up, but slipped on a wet stone and dropped him. After a lot of strain, he picked the man up and carried him to town. *(end)*

SUPER-CHRISTIAN TO THE RESCUE!

Here is a series of short vignettes, which can be adapted or changed as you see fit. They deal with common problems that kids have, such as understanding parents, depression, and discouragement. In each case, Super-Christian *(dressed in a superhero costume)* comes dashing in to shed some light on the subject. It's a fun way to teach biblical truths.

You might want to create several more of these and feature one each week at your youth meeting. For example, at some time during each meeting, Super-Christian arrives "just in the nick of time." The kids will laugh as well as learn something.

SCENE ONE:

Daughter: *(runs on stage—her bedroom)* Oh, Mom, you never trust me! You never let me do the things I want to do. I always have to follow your rules or Dad's rules or Gramma's rules or my teacher's rules. I never get to do what I want to do!

Mom: *(entering room)* Mary Beth, don't walk away from me when I am talking to you! Why is it whenever we have an argument, you run to your room to cry like a baby? If you're so grown up, why don't you talk to me, instead of throwing a tantrum!

Daughter: When I do talk, you never listen! It's like you turn off your ears. You just stand there with your arms crossed and nod your head just like you're doing now. You lay down the law and expect me to obey you, and you don't listen to my feelings at all!

Mom: Mary Beth, try to understand that the rules, as you call them, are there to protect you, to teach you right from wrong. You are too young to be going to a high school party, and those kids are too wild. I'm afraid of the things that go on—the drugs, the alcohol. You don't need that kind of temptation!

Daughter: You are so unfair! So mean! I wouldn't do anything stupid! I don't want to do drugs, I just want to be with my friends and have fun. Stop treating me like a child!

Mom: But you *are* a child, and as long as you are a child in my house, you will do as I say!

Someone in the audience: This looks like a job for Super-Christian! *(Super-Christian enters with theme song playing. He trips on the stage as he enters.)*

Super-C: Well, here I am. Ready to save the day! What's the problem here?

Mom: Ralph, what are you doing in that ridiculous outfit?

Super-C: I'm not Ralph. I'm that awesomely handsome, wise, and wonderful superhero who rescues people who are in distress! And I've come to open your eyes through the power of God to help you find a solution to your problem!

Daughter: All right, Ralph. What do you and God have to say about Mom not trusting me, not listening to me, and not letting me have any fun?

Super-C:	Mom, you love Mary Beth, right? And Mary Beth, you love Mom, right? Well, that's the answer, right there. No need to thank me—
Mom:	Wait a minute. You want to run that by me again in slow motion so I can understand?
Super-C:	Sure. Because you love each other, you can help each other understand how you feel. But you don't have to fight about it. Just listen when the other speaks. Mom, if you really love Mary Beth, you won't need rules to protect her. Your love will teach her right from wrong. And you can trust her because through your love you have taught her how to make a choice and how to accept the consequences.
	Mary Beth, if you really love Mom, you'd see that she is just trying to help you grow. She doesn't want you to get hurt. You've got to try and accept her way, because God chose her to be your teacher. If you both listen to each other, you'll be able to work out a compromise. *(He exits with the theme music playing.)*
Mom:	I'm sorry, Mary Beth. I'll try to be a better listener. If you want to go to that party, you can, but you have to be home by eleven.
Daughter:	I'm sorry, too. And I'll try to listen better to you. Actually, I don't think I'll go to that party anyway. I think I'll just stay home and pick on Ralph. Hey, where did he go, anyway?

SCENE TWO:

Tim:	*(lonely guy, on stage sitting on a chair, speaking to the audience)* Did you ever have one of those days when you feel like crawling under a rock, like hiding in the closet, like folding yourself up like a letter and stuffing yourself in an envelope and mailing yourself to the North Pole and getting lost in the mail? Well, that's exactly how I feel. I just got my science exam back. I got a 37. I can't believe it, a 37! I'm going to die. The only 37 in the class. Why do I even bother going to school? And to top that off, I just found out I didn't make the soccer team. And get this—my mom told me I'm going to have to wear braces and my best friend is moving to Tazmania! My dog is even growling at me. My father cut my allowance. I mean, talk about a rough life, you're looking at the king of losers!

Someone in Audience: This looks like a job for Super-Christian! *(He enters running through the audience and yelling.)*

Super-C: Here I come to save the day! I heard about all your bad luck and I just wanted to cheer you up.

Tim: Even your silly costume won't cheer me up. I'm a zero . . . washed up . . . finished . . . a failure . . . kaput!

Super-C: Hey, don't give up. There have been people worse off than you who still found lots to be thankful for! Why I know a guy who was betrayed by a good friend, whipped, laughed at, spit upon, and eventually killed just because he didn't fit in.

Tim: God.

Super-C: That's right! And you know even after that, he rose above all those horrible things and forgave all the people who hurt him. He knew that even dying wasn't going to stop him. Now he is honored and praised by people all over the world. Now, don't you think if that guy made it through all that suffering that you could make it through your run of hard times! After all, Jesus said he would be with you always—even when the going gets rough.

Tim: Yeah, you're right. I guess I was just drowning in self-pity. Thanks for the rescue.

Super-C: *(They walk off together.)* Come on, let's go get a Coke down at the 7-Eleven. Sorry about the soccer team. I never was much good at it either. Why don't we go practice together a little later.

SCENE THREE:

Girl: *(runs out, looks all over the stage for something)* Now where could I have put it? I'm always losing it. Maybe it's over there. *(goes into audience, looks for it, and asks one of the audience)* Hey, have you seen it? No, you won't know where it is. Nobody knows what happened to it!

Youth Director: What are you doing? You are interrupting our meeting. Why don't you look for whatever you lost after the meeting is over?

Girl: I can't! I can't sit down at a time like this! I'm so depressed. Maybe I should sit down and think about it. Then I'll remember where I lost it! *(sits on stage)*

Youth Director:	Well, this looks like a job for Super-Christian! *(shouts)* YO! SUPER-CHRISTIAN! YOU'RE ON!
Super-C:	*(enters with theme music)* Ta Da! Here I am to save the day! What's the problem? Where's the problem? *(looks around)*
Girl:	Oh, it's not here anywhere! I can't find it.
Super-C:	Mind if I ask what it is you're looking for?
Girl:	Well, let me describe it for you. It's kind of big and strong and comes in handy when you're feeling hopeless. Like I am right now. Some people have a lot of it. Some people have just a little, like about the size of a grain of mustard seed. But it will grow if you let it. Unfortunately, I just lost mine.
Super-C:	H'm. I don't get it.
Girl:	My faith, dummy! I've lost my faith and I can't find it anywhere. I've looked to my friends, my family, my church, in the closet, under my bed, and even in here. And so far, I've come up empty.
Super-C:	Have you looked in your . . . heart? Or in the Bible? Have you looked to Jesus?
Girl:	My heart is empty. I don't understand Bible talk and I can't see Jesus. How can I believe in someone I can't see?
Super-C:	That's what your faith is all about! Believing that Jesus is your friend and Savior, the one who will fill your heart and help you understand his Word. Let me share some of my faith with you. And together, we can help yours to grow.

THE TATOR FAMILY

This skit deals with personality types. There are no lines to learn, but each participant should try to act out his or her part according to the descriptions as read by the narrator. Props and actions are left entirely up to your own imagination. Each character can be introduced to the audience, and then a discussion can follow.

Here are the members of the Tator family:

Speck Tator: He likes to watch everyone else rather than get involved in anything personally. He is always on the outside looking in. He is usually expert at evaluating and helps those who are participating by cheering them on. But because Speck has the advantage of watching from the stands, he can also make unrealistic assessments from a distance and be quite fickle with his support.

Dick Tator: Dick doesn't consult anyone. He makes all his decisions by himself and sees others only as means to accomplish his will. Dick usually gets high marks for getting things done, but low marks for working with others.

Agi Tator: Whenever things get dull, Agi is always there to stir things up. She is often a nuisance, but many times keeps everyone on their toes by disturbing the comfortable status quo.

Hesi Tator: It is very difficult for Hesi to make decisions. She always needs just a little bit more information before making a decision. If and when Hesi does make a decision, however, it has usually been thought through carefully.

Emmy Tator: Emmy is a follower and can easily become a hero worshiper. Heavily influenced by those around her, Emmy's future is determined by the kinds of people she patterns her life after.

Common Tator: Common always has advice or criticism on any subject. Always talking and always very authoritative sounding, he often sounds like he knows what he is talking about, but usually doesn't.

Irri Tator: Irri is a twin of Agi with a mean streak in her. She likes to stir things up just for the sake of causing confusion and disarray. She is abrasive and even when she takes the correct position on a subject, still winds up alienating those around her.

Vegi Tator: Some call Vegi lazy because she just sits around doing nothing. She doesn't take any risks and tends to take what's given without giving anything in return. But at least Vegi is predictable and somewhat stable.

Devis Tator:	Devis is a revolutionary. He believes in confrontation, radical change. It is his philosophy that the only way to change something is to destroy it and start all over. Devis is weak on alternatives or ideas for rebuilding, and considers that someone else's job.
Facili Tator:	Facili is warm and personable. She is almost selfless. She works hard at enabling others to become better. She is a good listener and asks the kinds of questions that allow people to speak about things that matter to them. But Facili can sometimes be a nuisance because she sees every gathering as an opportunity to use her gifts and sometimes she just needs to let her abilities remain dormant.
Cogi Tator:	Cogi is a thinker. She is different from her brother Medi because Cogi thinks deeply about matters that will affect the way she acts. She weighs everything carefully before acting and attempts to make sure she has considered all the alternatives.
Medi Tator:	Medi thinks deeply and finds satisfaction in the act itself. His thinking never really leads to any constructive action, however. It is the act of pondering that matters to Medi and not the content.
Roe Tator:	Roe is a systems man. He believes that everyone should have their turn regardless of qualification. He is task oriented and is only involved as long as the task is his responsibility. He believes in change for change's sake and doesn't like to remain in one spot too long.

TODAY?

Here's a great skit that deals with the second coming of Christ from heaven's perspective. You may want an introductory or concluding text: 1 Thessalonians 5:1–12.

Characters:	Michael, the angel
	Gabriel, the angel
	Abraham

Peter
David

Scene: A table sits in the middle of the stage with a box representing an earth scanner on it. A phone sits on the table also. Michael stands behind or beside the scanner adjusting knobs.

Michael: *(Telephone rings.)* Uh-oh, it's the hotline. *(Answers phone.)* Yes sir, good morning. Today? Right now? But nobody is expecting it! *(pause)* Right sir, they are supposed to be watching and prepared, and a few are, but . . . yes, sir . . . yes . . . right away, sir. *(Dials phone.)* Hello, Dave? Get the troops ready. Today is C-day! Yes, I mean today!

Gabriel: *(enters singing "Oh What a Beautiful Morning" and struts around during the following conversation, but hardly ever looks at Michael)* Well, Michael, I see things are in order this morning.

Michael: Gabriel, my friend, you better get your lips tuned up and your trumpet polished.

Gabriel: These lips are always tuned. Always ready to sound forth the call of God.

Michael: Well, you . . .

Gabriel: Always in tune for the Lord.

Michael: Then you are already . . .

Gabriel: Always polished up and ready to blow is the trumpet of this angel.

Michael: Then you'll be glad to hear that today is the day.

Gabriel: *(not listening to Michael)* My troops of trumpeters always stand with horns ready to blow forth the call of God, whenever that may be . . . TODAY? It can't be! I'm not ready! I have to practice. I don't even remember how to blow charge. My troops aren't ready. Are you sure it's today? How could it be?

Michael: That's what the Almighty said. I just talked to him on the hotline.

Gabriel: Man, I better get ready. *(hurries out, runs into Abraham)*

Abraham: *(entering)* Morning, Gabe, what's the hurry?

Gabriel: I'm not ready!

Abraham: What's with him? What's he mean he's not ready?

Michael: Not ready for the C-day.

Abraham: Really? I thought everybody was ready for that day. When it comes I'll be ready. But that will probably be a good while.

Michael: I don't know, Abraham. It could be sooner.

Abraham: What do you mean? I thought a bunch of signs had to occur first.

Michael: Suppose they already have.

Abraham: Maybe, but I just don't think Jehovah would do it yet. See, I figure there is going to be this war between Russia and . . .

Michael: Abe, I got a call from the Almighty a little while ago. He said he's decided upon a day.

Abraham: When, Mike? You gotta tell me!

Michael: Today.

Abraham: TODAY? It can't be! I'm not ready. I've got to get my people ready! I've got to get all Israel together. I gotta find Moses and Aaron. *(exit)*

Peter: *(entering)* Hey, Mike, what's with Abraham? You'd think today was the second coming or something.

Michael: Maybe it is, Peter.

Peter: *(ignoring Michael)* Everybody is getting kind of stirred. I saw Gabe practicing his trumpet. He hasn't blown that thing in years. I guess it could be soon.

Michael: Peter, it's today.

Peter: Yeah, it could be anytime soon . . . WHAT? TODAY? It can't be. Why didn't he warn us?

Michael: What do you mean? He did.

Peter: I've got to get the gates ready. They have to be polished. I have to wash my robe. I gotta get out the Book of Life. I thought it would be soon but not today! *(runs out)* Hey, Andrew, Thomas!

David: *(enters)* How's it look, General?

Michael: Real good, Dave. There's a bit of confusion, but things are shaping up. Are the troops in line?

David: Ready to go.

Michael: Good. We've got just a few minutes to countdown.

David: Say, Michael, do you think there's going to be enough room for all those people in heaven? You know they're still working on those mansions over on the west side.

Michael: The Lord knows what he's doing. Besides, there's going to be fewer than we expected. I've been watching the earth scanner. It looks like we aren't the only ones surprised and unprepared. There's going to be even more confusion on earth.

David: I sure hope we get a lot of kids. I'd hate to see them go . . .

Michael:	Right. Me, too.
David:	I better get to the troops.
Michael:	I'll be right there. *(picks up phone)* Yes, this is General Michael. Get ready for the countdown. *(pause)* Ready . . . one minute . . . 59 . . . 58 . . . 57 . . . *(pause, looking down at earth scanner)* Ready or not, here we come. *(exit)*

TOM MEETS GOD

Here's a good skit to deal with the topic of The Cost of Discipleship. There are three characters, although the person who plays God could be offstage so that only his voice is heard. The setting is heaven.

Tom:	*(knocks and an angel opens the door)* Hi! My name is Tom. I would like to see the person in charge, please.
Angel:	Sure, come on in.
Tom:	Look, uh, I know this guy is really important, but do you think he would see someone like me?
Angel:	He sees everyone. You can see him any time you'd like.
Tom:	Could I see him now?
Angel:	Go right on in.
Tom:	Now?
Angel:	Yes.
Tom:	*(hesitating and then slowly walking in)* Uh, excuse me, my name is Tom. I wondered if I could see you for a few minutes?
God:	My name is God and I've got all the time you need.
Tom:	Well, I'm going to high school right now, and I am a little confused about what I should do. A couple of my friends say you can help, but they seem just as confused as I am. To be quite honest, I haven't really been impressed by your work. I mean, don't get me wrong, my friends are really good friends, you know, and they really seem to like me, but they haven't got it so good. Bob, one of my friends, his dad is an alcoholic and my other friends' folks are getting a divorce. The crazy thing is my folks are great, I really love them, everything's going great except . . . except I can't

seem to see the point in life. In spite of all the junk that is happening to my friends, they really seem to be convinced that you are important. So that's why I'm here. I just thought you could give me some pointers. I just feel kinda lost.

God: My price is high.

Tom: That's O.K., because my folks are pretty well off. What is it?

God: All.

Tom: All?

God: Yes, All. Everything.

Tom: Sheesh. Don't you have a lay-a-way plan? How about a pay as you go? Isn't your profit margin a little out of line?

God: Actually, my cost was quite high also . . . ask my Son.

Tom: Well, uh, I think I'll have to wait awhile. I appreciate your taking the time to talk to me and I'm sure you're worth it; it's just that at my age, it's a little too soon to give up everything. After all, when you're young that's when the good times happen. Besides, I think I can get what I'm looking for at a much cheaper price.

God: Be careful, Tom. The price may be cheaper, but your cost may be much higher than you think.

Tom: Yeah, sure. Well, nice talking to you, God. Maybe I'll see you around some time.

God: Yes, Tom, and there's no maybe about it.

THE TOMB REVISITED

This is a modern version of the Easter story. Not very appropriate for a solemn morning service, but great as a creative way to introduce a story everyone seems overfamiliar with. Good discussion possibilities.

SCENE I

Setting: Four guards are sleeping in front of the tomb of Jesus. They are to snore and awaken without paying any attention to the tomb.

Louie: *(wakes up, rubs eyes, yawns and stretches)* Man is it cold out here—I better build a fire. *(begins to rub two sticks, puts wood and leaves together, blows into it, etc.)*

Bernie:	Hey, whatcha doing, Louie?
Louie:	Oh, just putting my Boy Scout training to use.
Bernie:	Forgot the matches again, eh? (gets up and goes over to a knapsack and finds a box of matches) Here ya go. (throws matches to Louie)
Marvin:	(awakens from sleep) Hey, what's going on with all the noise?
Louie:	(testily) I'm trying to get a fire going for breakfast.
Marvin:	Never mind for me—I've got mine all ready to go. (shows a box of cereal and begins to prepare his own breakfast)
Norman:	(who has by this time also awakened, sniffs in the air as if something is burning) Hey, what's burning?
Louie:	Probably wood.
Norman:	(walking toward fire) No, no. It smells like something rotten is burning. (pause)
Bernie:	Oh, it's just your imagination.
Marvin:	No, I smell something now, too.
Louie:	What's that in the fire there? (pokes a stick in the fire and pulls out a burned shoe)
Norman:	Those are my new Adidas you've been using for kindling wood, you idiot. Why, I ought to strangle you with my bare . . . (This last line is said while chasing Louie around the fire. Louie falls at Norman's knees, wraps his arms around him, and begs for mercy.)
Louie:	Please, Norman, have mercy on me.
Bernie & Marvin:	Yeah Norman, give him a break.
Norman:	(Just then Norman notices the empty tomb. His eyes are large with astonishment.) Look! The tomb! It's empty!
Everyone:	We're in big trouble.
Marvin:	We are all gonna get fired.
Louie:	(crying) I'm going to lose my pension, and I only had three more years to go until retirement.
Bernie:	Don't feel bad, I've got a house to pay for and a son attending Jerusalem State Medical School.
Norman:	What are you guys talking about? It's not our fault that the tomb is empty. Jesus must have really come back from the dead, just as he predicted.

Louie:	What makes you say that, Norman?
Norman:	Well, that rock. It's moved. Who do you think moved it? The tooth fairy?
Marvin:	(glaring at Bernie) I'm sure we would have slept through an earthquake.
Bernie:	Well, don't look at me. I don't know where Jesus is.
Louie:	Well if it's not our fault that he's gone, let's get down to headquarters and tell the chief priests to put out an APB.
Everyone:	Right! (picking up sleeping bags, putting out fire, etc. as curtain closes)

SCENE II

Setting:	A room with a desk and chairs, depicting the place of the chief priests.
Chief Priest Caiaphas:	(excitedly) What are you guys doing here? You're supposed to be at the tomb!
Louie:	(nonchalantly) There's nothing there to guard. Jesus is gone.

Chief Priest Annas:	*(very excitedly)* Gone! Where did he go?
Marvin:	Norman thinks that Jesus has risen from the dead, just like he predicted he would.
Chief Priest Annas:	*(to all)* You nincompoops! We can't have people believing Jesus came back from the dead. Think what it will do to our religion and more importantly, all of our jobs! Why, who is going to give to the temple if they think there is a risen Savior?
Bernie:	Well, what do you want us to do?
Chief Priest Caiaphas:	Let us think about it for a minute. *(Caiaphas and Annas huddle for a few moments.)*
Both:	*(from the middle of the huddle)* That's a good idea.
Chief Priest Caiaphas:	*(coming back to the guards)* Look. Who else knows about Jesus rising from the dead?
All the guards:	Nobody.
Chief Priest Caiaphas:	*(rubbing his hands together)* All right, this is what we are going to say to the press. Quote: "We do not know the whereabouts of the body of Jesus of Nazareth because while the guards were sleeping, his disciples stole him away."
Norman:	That's no good. If we were sleeping, how would we know his disciples stole the body?
Chief Priest Annas:	*(testily)* Look Norman, we are doing this for *you* as well as ourselves. This statement will not only save your job but will also make you rich.
Norman:	*(sarcastically)* How?
Chief Priest Annas:	*(pulls out a wad of money)* This money is for you if you can keep our little secret. Do I have any takers, boys?
Bernie:	*(greedily stuffs money in his pockets)* I've got a boy in medical school.
Louie:	I need a little extra for my retirement. *(stuffing money into his pockets)*
Marvin:	Everybody likes money.
Norman:	*(firmly)* Money never brought a man back from the dead though. *(exits right leaving the others standing in the room with a dumb look on their faces)*

WHOLE ARMOR OF GOD

This skit is a mime that involves two people—the new Christian and Satan. It is based on Ephesians 6:10–16. A narrator can help set the scene.

This skit is quite effective without any props, as long as the Christian knows what piece of armor he has on and anything goes with the crafty Devil. The pieces of armor are the following: Helmet of Salvation, Belt of Truth, Breastplate of Righteousness, Feet Shod with the Readiness of the Gospel, Shield of Faith, and finally, the Sword of the Spirit.

One person puts on armor, one piece at a time, as the narrator tells a story of a fencing match between a new Christian and Satan. The new Christian starts out each day with an additional piece of armor. The same thing happens each time: Satan attacks in an area that isn't covered with protective armor. The results are all the same: The Christian returns home tired and wounded. He finally goes out with the whole armor of God and puts up a very good fight. Just as the Devil is about to win again, the narrator reminds him that he forgot his sword. The Christian draws a fake sword and says, "Greater is he that is in me, than he that is in the world." Satan runs away and the Christian relates that the Word of God as a sword will triumph over the evil one.

WHOSE BIRTHDAY IS IT?

This is a good discussion-starter to use during the Christmas holidays. It features a family of four—Mom and Dad, their son Ken, and daughter Pam. Of course, you can add as many characters as you wish. The setting is a typical living room on Christmas morning.

After the skit, discuss what happened with the family. See how long it takes for the group to make the connection between this family's ignoring Pam's birthday and how we often ignore the birthday of Christ.

Pam: *(complaining)* No birthday present again. Why did I have to be born on Christmas Day? Did you know that nobody has ever remembered my birthday?

Ken: Considering the time of year, who's going to remember a mere birthday? It's Christmas!

Pam: *(complaining even more)* You get birthday presents every year, and so do Dad and Mom. But all I ever get is combination birthday/Christmas presents. It's not fair!

Dad: *(Dad and Mom enter.)* Merry Christmas, Pam. Merry Christmas, Ken.

Ken: Merry Christmas, Dad, Mom.

Pam: It's also my birthday, you know.

Mom: We know, dear. Merry Christmas.

Dad: Well, let's all open presents, shall we?

Mom: I wonder what I got from Santa this year!

Ken: Here, Dad! *(handing him a gift)* Open this one!

The characters ad-lib their parts for a while, with Mom, Dad, and Ken continuing to be enthusiastic about opening Christmas gifts and Pam becoming more and more upset that her birthday is being ignored. Finally, Pam bursts into tears and leaves the room. The others act surprised and annoyed that Pam is making such a big deal over such a "little" thing.

Ken: I wonder what's gotten into her! What a Scrooge.

THE WITNESS

This short skit will raise some interesting questions about the subject of Witnessing.

Script: The lights come up on a typical student union. Joe is seated at a table studying in preparation for an upcoming test. Nick, a super straight-looking student, approaches and sits right next to Joe, ignoring the empty seats around him.

Nick: Hi. How ya doin'? Do you live around here?

Joe: *(eyes still on books)* Yeah.

Nick: Where? Where do you live?

Joe: *(still reading)* In the dorms.

Nick: Really? I thought about living there once. What's it like? *(Joe doesn't answer.)* Do you study here all the time?

Joe: *(With his concentration finally broken, he gives Nick a hard look.)* Yes, I study here a lot because over in the dorms too many people bother me and I can't concentrate!

Nick:	Yeah, it must be really hard to study with people bothering you all the time.
Joe:	Yes, it is!
Nick:	*(begins talking faster, acts rather nervous and unsure)* Are you saved?
Joe:	What?
Nick:	Are you saved? You see, I belong to the Go With God Student Christian Club, and we are sort of taking a survey to see who is going to hell. But you don't have to go to hell. *(Nick pulls out a booklet called "God wants You!")* Right here in this little book is a chance for you to have eternal life. Here on page one it says, "You are hiding from God in the wretchedness of your ugly sins. You must repent—"
Joe:	*(He is dumbfounded and speechless until this point.)* Wait a minute.
Nick:	Oh, please save your questions until I've read you the whole thing.
Joe:	In case it's not obvious, I'm trying to study.
Nick:	There are only three more pages. Now this verse from the Bible . . .
Joe:	*(louder)* I am not interested in your weird religious ideas!
Nick:	*(pause)* What's your name?

Joe:	My name isn't important. Will you please go away so I can study?
Nick:	If you don't listen to me, your name, whatever it is, won't be written in the Book of Life and—
Joe:	*(Very mad, he explodes.)* Look! I am trying to study, or are you too ignorant to see that. What is it with you Jesus Freaks anyway? Do you work on a commission basis? One more star in your halo for every soul saved! Well, I'm not interested, so flake off!
Nick:	*(pause, dead serious)* He said we would be persecuted.
Joe:	*(resigned)* I don't believe this! *(He slams book shut, rips booklet in half, throws it in Nick's face and storms off mumbling something about crazy fanatics. The lights fade, all except a large pool of light down center stage. Nick rises and enters pool of light.)*

Mr. Applegate:	*(from the darkness behind Nick)* That was very good, Nick.
Nick:	*(His whole composure changed to a strong determined person.)* That wasn't just "very good."
Mr. Applegate:	*(He comes into the light with Nick. He wears a dark business suit, and there is something ominous about him.)* How do you mean?
Nick:	That was the best you've ever seen. I know it, you know it, and Number One knows it.

Mr. Ap͏̱ ᵃate:	That's why I have come to talk to you. Number One has a new assignment for you.
Nick:	It's about time.
Mr. Applegate:	There is a new church and coffeehouse that has just opened on the north side. The man who runs it has a very intimate relationship with the Enemy. He is very dangerous and could change our whole standing there without some fast action. Number One seems to think that you are creative enough to come up with some good moves. We'll start you as a heroin pusher, but if you can't work with that let us know and other arrangements can be made. Can you handle it?
Nick:	I can.
Mr. Applegate:	Good. Let me warn you Nick, we don't usually let demons of your standing take a job like this. If you fail, well, you know what will happen.
Nick:	I know.
Mr. Applegate:	Very well. You'll start right away.

WITNESSING, AMERICAN STYLE

Here's another good skit that deals with the subject of witnessing. Three characters are needed; the only prop, a park bench (or a reasonable facsimile).

Characters:	Derk Bobby Snodgrass Sam Schmuck
Derk:	*(He is dressed casually with sack lunch in one hand and paperback book in other hand, horn-rimmed glasses in pocket. He enters, sits down on a park bench, and begins to eat lunch.)* What a lovely day! *(He takes out glasses and begins to read the book.)*
Bobby:	*(He is dressed in pastoral suit and tie and carries a copy of Christianity Today. He enters, sits down on one side of Derk, and begins to read after he says the following to Derk.)* What a lovely day!

Sam: (*He is dressed very businesslike in a three-piece suit and tie and carries a briefcase. He enters, sits down on other side of Derk, and opens his briefcase. He takes out Bible, pad, and pen.*) What a lovely day! (*He says to Derk as he begins to read and study Bible. Silence ensues for several moments as each one does his own thing and tries to ignore the others. Tension climaxes and finally Sam breaks the silence.*) The poor spiritually starving world, they don't read the Bible and feed on its life-sustaining truths.

Bobby: (*He is oblivious to what Sam said, obviously reading an article on world hunger.*)

Derk: (*He is a little perturbed that his privacy has been invaded.*) The poor starving American. Someone is sitting on his lunch! (*He pulls his sack lunch out from under Bobby.*)

Sam: (*There is silence for another moment. Sam happens to look up and recognize Bobby.*) Bobby, is that you?

Bobby: (*He looks up startled.*) Why, Sam, is that you?

Sam: Well, Bobby Snodgrass, it's really you!

Bobby: Well, Sam, Sammy Schmuck, I do declare! (*They both rise and embrace, squishing Derk.*) Well, how've ya been? (*He sits down on Derk's lunch again.*)

Sam: Fine, and you?

Bobby: Good. The last time I saw you was five years ago when we graduated from Bible college together.

Sam: Yeah. Never forget those times at good old P.C. Say, what ya been up to since then?

Bobby: Well, ya know, the Lord has really been blessing me. After graduation I had an interview with Pastor Rippensteimer from First Church, and he took me on staff there, and that's where I've been ever since.

Sam: Naw, you're kidding! Not First Church on Main St., the one that seats five thousand people!

Bobby: That's the one. You know the Lord really knows how to bless his people if we'll sell out completely to him. By the way, what've you been doin'?

(*Meanwhile Derk has given up trying to read his book and pulled his sack lunch out from under Bobby, and attempts to ignore the two talking over him. He pulls out a flattened sandwich and disgustedly throws it back into the sack.*)

Sam: Well, you know how I've always wanted to travel as an evangelist and sing and preach the gospel all over the country?

Bobby: Yeah.

Sam: Well, after graduation I contacted Billy Braham, and he took me on as his assistant.

Bobby: Naw, not THE famous evangelist—Billy Braham?

Sam: Yep! That's the one. You know I can't get over how greatly the Lord will use his servants if we will really commit ourselves to his work.

Derk: *(Meanwhile Derk has tried to return to reading his book but has trouble keeping it out of the way of the flying gestures of the other two as they talk.)*

Sam: Speaking of his work, guess how many people we have won to the Lord in the last two years?

Bobby: How many?

Sam: Almost two thousand!

Bobby: *(competitively)* Yeah? Well, guess how much First Church has grown in the last two years?

Sam: How much?

Bobby: We've added almost three thousand new members!

Derk: *(Meanwhile Derk has given up on trying to read the book and pulled out his lunch again. This time, to his horror, he pulls out a flattened orange!)*

Sam: WOW! I see the Lord's been blessing you, too! You know it's amazing how many people the Holy Spirit will draw to himself when you come right out and tell people what they've gotta do. Turn or burn—it's that simple.

Bobby: Well, you know Pastor Rippensteimer is a real pro at giving altar calls and his philosophy is love. You've got to show people the love of God! Then they'll want to get saved.

Sam: Naw, man. You've got to put a little fear in their hearts. You gotta make 'em feel the hellfire and brimstone or they won't even respond.

Bobby: That's no way to share the *Good News*. You can't scare them into the kingdom! You gotta love 'em in like Jesus did. *(Derk looks back and forth at each one as they argue the point.)*

Sam: No way. That doesn't work on the twentieth-century mind-set. You got to come right out and tell them where they're headed, like the prophets did in the old testament.

Bobby: *(He gets upset.)* That isn't what the Bible says. The Bible says you have to have love.

Sam: Oh yeah, where's that found?

Bobby: Uh, Hezariah 3:16.

Sam: Well, I can show you right here in . . . in . . . *(turning pages of Bible)* in the gospel of Moses where it says, "with the rod I will chasten my people."

(Derk is getting squished more and more as Bob and Sam get hotter and hotter.)

Bobby: You always did have a hard time in our classes on interpreting the Bible.

Sam: Well, I remember the time you flunked out of Christian Doctrine 101!

Bobby: Why you no good, low down—

Sam: *(interrupts)* You hypocritical, good for nothing . . . *(They go for each other's throats and catch Derk in between them.)*

Bobby: *(He finally comes to his senses, releases Sam's neck.)* Hey man, what are we doing?

Sam: *(He releases Bobby's neck.)* I don't know, I guess we just got a little carried away. I'm sorry, man.

Bobby: Me, too.

Derk: *(He fell to the ground after the two stopped choking each other, picked himself up, and straightened his glasses. Finally after they finish apologizing, he talks.)* Hey, guys, could you tell me a little more about this Good News you've been talking about?

Bobby: Uh, I'm late for an appointment, I've gotta run.

Sam: Yeah, I just remembered, uh, I've gotta go to the bathroom. I'll see ya later, Bobby.

Bobby: Sure, good-by Sam. Good seein' ya Bro'.

Sam: You, too, Bobby, Lord bless ya. *(The two exit the same way they came in.)*

Derk: Man, some Good News!

WOULD YOU BELIEVE . . . ?

Here's a fun skit that deals with the topic of Faith. It can be used effectively with a lesson or study on Matthew 12:38–40.

Characters: Angel (dressed in normal human clothing)
              Man

An angel accidentally appears to a man on earth.

Angel: *(stumbles in.)* Man! That was some time-warp. I gotta be more careful where I step. *(looks around)* Wonder where I am?

Man: *(enters)* Hey, what are you doing in here? How'd you get in here?

Angel: *(looks around and behind him)* Me?

Man: *(sarcastically)* No, I was talking to that wall. Who else would I be talking to?

Angel: But . . . but you can't see me.

Man: What?

Angel: I'm invisible.

Man: *(sarcastically)* Oh! An invisible man? Well, we get all kinds around here.

Angel: This is crazy. You're not supposed to be able to see me . . . or hear me, either.

Man: *(even more sarcastically)* Well, I guess your magic potion wore off.

Angel: It's not a potion. You see, I'm . . . I'm not a man. I'm . . .

Man: Oh!

Angel: Really! I'm an angel.

Man: Is that right? Well, you certainly don't look like an angel to me. Where's your wings?

Angel: Look, I must have stumbled into a weird time-warp and ended up here by accident. I've always heard that when angels appear to men they look like men. That's the only form you could perceive, of course.

Man: Man, are you looney! I gotta get your tail out of here before I start believing you.

Angel: Listen, friend, you've got to help me get back to the spirit world. I was just on my way back to a new assignment—my first human. I used to only work with animals. I was in charge of skunks. Can you believe it? Am I glad that's over! I remember one time—

Man: Look, buddy, if you don't get out of here, I'm gonna have to call the police.

Angel: But you don't understand. I have to go out the same way I came in—through the time-warp that is connected to this room.

Man: Well, go ahead and fly out, Mr. Angel.

Angel: You still don't believe me.

Man: Why should I? You haven't done anything angelic.

Angel: What do you expect? A miracle?

Man: Now that wouldn't be a bad idea.

Angel: You humans are all alike.

Man: Well?

Angel: Oh! *(disgusted)* O.K. But this is strictly unauthorized procedure. Uh, how about if I tell you what you are thinking just now? You are wanting to get rid of me so you can go downstairs and talk to Miss Wells, a secretary in this building. Uh, wait, there's more. You're thinking about what she is wearing today. You, uh, you're having other thoughts, but I refuse to speak of them. *(pause)* Well, was that satisfactory?

Man: I've seen people mind read before. Now if you could get me a date with Miss Wells, that would be a miracle.

Angel: I'm afraid I don't have time for that. I noticed you seem to be quite thirsty. How about something cool and refreshing?

Man: Sure. *(Water flies in from offstage, hitting Man.)*

Angel: *(smiling)* Sorry, I forgot the cup. *(Cup flies in.)* Would you care for something to eat?

Man: No! No, that's fine. Listen, how about a different kind of miracle?

Angel: Sir, I'm afraid I can't stand here all day to work miracles for you. You've just got to believe me.

Man: Just one more.

Angel: I think you should know that the greatest sign you could want has already been given you.

Man: What are you talking about?

Angel: The greatest miracle in the world was when Jesus Christ died and God raised him back to life.

Man: But how can you expect me to believe that? I didn't see it happen.

Angel: You don't have to see it. All you have to do is believe it. *(pause)* Hey, something is happening to me. I feel like I'm being pulled away. *(falls off stage)*

Man: *(thinking)* You know, one good miracle and I might have believed him. *(shrugs and exits)*

Index of Subjects

Acts 3
Bible Broadway, 17

Attendance
Attendance Is a Little Down Tonight, 15

Body of Christ
The Body Life Skit, 21
Brother Hood Hour, 24
Gifts of Beauty, 54

Christian Love
Parable of the Shapes, 139
The Guest, 63

Christian Service
Disciple Auditions, 40
The Everlasting Invitational Track Meet, 45
Excuses, 47
Not Guilty?, 118
Sayin', Doin', or Bein', 148
Tom Meets God, 169

Christmas
Christmas on the Network News, 33
The Department Store Window, 43
The Guest, 63
He's Going to What?, 70
The Innkeeper's Wife, 78
Laney Looks at the Christmas Story, 89
Mary's Story, 107
Whose Birthday Is It?, 174

Commitment
Attendance Is a Little Down Tonight, 15
Disciple Auditions, 40
The Everlasting Invitational Track Meet, 45
Excuses, 47
Not Guilty?, 118
The Sacrifice, 146

Conversion of Paul
Letters to Mama, 93

Creation and Science
Oops!, 134

Easter
The Execution, 52
LX Minutes, 98
The Night Before Easter, 116
The Tomb Revisited, 170

Ephesians 6
Whole Armor of God, 174

Evangelism
Microcosm, 113

Faith
Would You Believe?, 182

Giving
The Offering Skit, 132

Good Samaritan
Melody in S, 112
The Spontaneous Samaritan, 159

Healing
    Bible Broadway, 17

Hymns
    Songs of the Heart, 153

John 4
    Jesus Met a Woman, 82

John the Baptist
    John the Ready, 85

Joshua
    But Lord, Isn't That a Bit Showy?, 28

Language
    Oh God!, 132

Lord's Prayer
    If God Should Speak, 74

Missions
    Microcosm, 113

Palm Sunday
    Palm Sunday in the News, 136

Parent/Teen Relationships
    All in the Point of View, 13
    Grounded!, 57
    A Mad Late Date, 105

Passage of Time
    Growing Up, 59

Peer Pressure
    The Jerk, 80

Personalities
    The Tator Family, 164

Prayer
    God and the I.R.S., 55

Prodigal Son
    Melody in F, 111

Roles
    The Tator Family, 164

Second Coming of Christ
    Today?, 166

Salvation
    The Day That Changed My Life, 37

Spiritual Gifts
    The Body Life Skit, 21
    Brother Hood Hour, 24
    Gifts of Beauty, 54

Swearing
    Oh God!, 132

Teen Problems
    Super Christian to the Rescue!, 160

Witnessing
    The $64,000 Testimony, 149
    The Witness, 175
    Witnessing, American Style, 178

Woman at the Well
    Jesus Met a Woman, 82

Worldly Values
    The Jerk, 80

Worship
    Songs of the Heart, 152

Zaccheus
    The Day That Changed My Life, 37